NE

MOTORWAYS

Affordable Alternatives
to Service Stations

Revised 11th Edition

by
Hugh Cantlie

Over 200 pubs, restaurants,
hotels and places of interest just
5 minutes off a motorway junction.

Published by Cheviot Books

1st Edition	Sep 2001	Reprint	Jan 2002
2nd Edition	Sep 2002	3rd Edition	Oct 2003
4th Edition	Oct 2004	5th Edition	Jan 2006
6th Edition	Feb 2007	7th Edition	Feb 2008
8th Edition	Apr 2010	Reprint	Sep 2010
2nd Reprint	Nov 2010	3rd Reprint	Dec 2010
9th Edition	Oct 2011	10th Edition	Nov 2012
Reprint	Oct 2012	2nd Reprint	Dec 2013
11th Edition	Jul 2014		

Copyright   Hugh Cantlie
Illustrations   Hugh Cantlie

Cheviot Books
e-mail: info@cheviotbooks.co.uk
website: www.cheviotbook.com
ISBN 978-09575602-08

Printed by Potts Print (UK), Cramlington

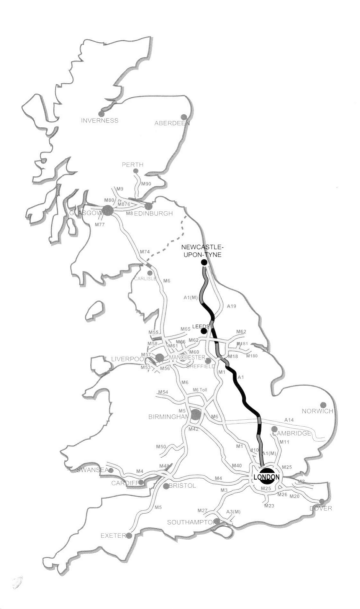

Contents

There are many reasons why there are changes and closures in this edition.

The main problem seems to be the inertia of the catering industry which is facing an increasingly changing world. The exceptions are the independent outlets and tenanted pubs who make the motorist welcome with personal attention - these have been included wherever possible.

It has become increasingly difficult to verify details such as the time for meals, as these seem to change from week to week. It would be advisable to check the times beforehand if you are on a tight schedule.

There is an increasing requirement for breakfast so in this edition we have majored in highlightng places which provide it, with an index on page 280.

We have also moved into the modern IT age so that those of you who have bought the Ebook version can download the information onto your Mobiles and Tablets.

Thanks are due to those who have helped with the production of this edition. They include entries who provided updates quickly and efficiently; Anthony Duke for his accurate maps and plans; Jacques Voepel for his IT input and special thanks to Caroline Stockton who helped with the driving and second opinions on the many places which were visited. Fantasy Prints helped to design the covers. Potts Print (UK) have again not only done the printing but Jonathan Clark and Clare Goddard moulded the raw material into shape.

Our thanks to all of you who have told us of your experiences or made suggestions for new inclusions.

Lastly, to help us all would you please take Near the Motorways in with you when having a meal en-route.

The guide has been arranged following the numerical order of the motorways. It starts with the A1, A14 and A19 and then the M1 through to the M90 which ends at Perth.

In the top panel of each page is the Motorway number in larger letters and then the Junction number with the names of towns and road numbers as they would appear on the Motorways signs.

There is then a text description on how to find the entry in case your Satnav has let you down. The plan, which also shows any Filling Stations, is helpful in case of need.
Where applicable there are names of Places of Interest nearby with an Index on pages 291 to 295 giving telephone numbers.

The letter in the roundel corresponds with that on the plan, followed by the name of the entry. Below is the address and to the right is the post code for Satnav purposes. The next line has the telephone number so you can book a table or confirm times of serving food, as well as checking if there is space for your caravan or horse box. The Website and E-mail is given below.

Times for food should be checked in case they have changed since going to print.

🛏	Number of bedrooms
☕	Coffee or teas
🪑	Ouside seating
♿	Disabled
👪	Children welcome
🐾	Dogs allowed
🍳	Breakfasts
£-£££	Price range

There is then a brief write-up to give a feeling of what to expect and above all whether it is friendly, efficient and has an imaginative menu.

The watercolours are apparently flattering.

A1
9	Three Horse Shoes
-	Hare & Hounds
-	Lion Hotel
16	Stilton Cheese
17	Crown Inn
17	Falcon
-	Welby Arms
34	White Swan
51	Green Dragon
65	Angel View Inn

A14
9	Overstone Arms
18	George Inn
25	Cock
26	King William IV

A19
	Oswalds
	Old Oak Tree

M1
22	Field Head Hotel
38	Old Post Office
47	Swan Hotel

M2
1	Leather Bottle
5	Harrow Inn

M3
9	Bush Inn

M4
13	Langley Hall Inn
14	Hare Restaurant
15	Plough Inn
15	Silks on the Downs
49	Bird in Hand

M5
9	Hobnails
19	The Priory
25	Globe Inn
30	Greendale Farm Shop

M6
12	Bell Inn
36	Crooklands Hotel
38	Old School House
40	Brantwood Hotel

M11
8	Three Willows
12	Rupert Brooke
12	Green Man
12	The Orchard

M18
6	John Bull

M20
7	Kings Head
9	Hare & Hounds
10	Honest Miller
11	Drum

M23
10	White Swan
11	Black Swan

M25
6	Bell Inn

M26
2	Vineyard

M40
6	Cherry Tree

M42
3	Portway

M61
8	Dressers Arms

M62
37	Wellington

M74
13	Abington Hotel
15	Ariete
15	Black Bull

M90
4	Baxters

A1
15	Abbotts Elm
17	Black Horse
17	Loch Fyne
-	William Cecil Hotel
-	Royal Oak
44	Arabian Horse
56	Black Bull
56	White Swan

A19
-	Bay Horse

M3
5	Mill House
9	Tichborne Arms

M4
14	Tally Ho
15	Parklands Hotel
16	Stanton Manor Hotel

M5
9	Theoc House
14	Gables Hotel
28	Five Bells
29	Darts Farm Shop

M6
17	Old Hall
36	Strickland Arms
36	Sizergh Farm Shop

M11
12	Burwash Manor Farm
12	Red Lion

M20
7	Black Horse
10	Blacksmiths Arms

M23
10	Old House Inn

M25
6	Godstone Hotel
6	Green Rooms

M40
6	Shepherds Crook
6	Swan
7	Plough
11	Limes Barn
11	Fox
12	Antelope

M42
9	Beehive

M54
4	Hundred House Hotel

M62
37	Bowmans

M74
15	Brodies

A1(M)

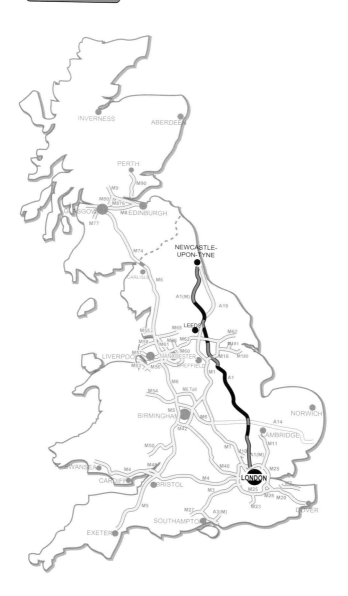

A1(M) London to Newcastle

LONDON TO NEWCASTLE

JUNCTIONS TO

The A1 is the old Great North Road from London to Edinburgh and for much of its length it still uses the routes of the old Roman roads.

It is being upgraded to motorway standard especially on the northern sections.

The upgrading from the M62 at Ferrybridge to Bedale has now been completed and work has started on the last link to Scotch Corner which is due to be finished by 2017.

As a result of these roadworks, which could cause delays, we have included the A19 from Thirsk to the Tyne Tunnel as an alternative route. It is a dual-carriageway as far as Newcastle but it does not have numbered junctions.

There are still stretches of dual carriageway to be upgraded such as from Baldock to Huntingdon and the long section from Peterborough to south of Doncaster.

These sections have been included although the turn-offs are not numbered and only have the names of the villages and towns. They are shown in grey to show the difference between dual carriageways and motorways.

For ease of use we have divided the A1 into five different sections. The first is from Hatfield to the junction with the A14 at Huntingdon; the second from Huntingdon to Grantham; the next is from Grantham to the M62 at Ferrybridge and then the section from there to Scotch Corner. The last part is the motorway to Newcastle.

 **A1(M)** LONDON TO NEWCASTLE

HATFIELD TO HUNTINGDON
TO INCLUDE JUNCTIONS 6 TO 13

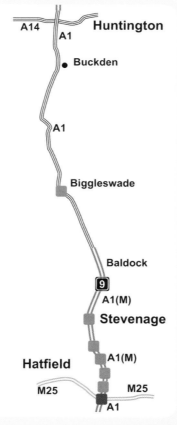

From the junction with the M25 at South Mimms, it is a motorway until north of Baldock. Hatfield is bypassed by going underneath it through a tunnel.

Welwyn Garden City was the first of the conceptual towns to be designed to bring the country to the town in the 1920s. It is still a surprisingly pleasant town to live in.

Stevenage was the first of the post-Second World War new towns. Apparently the brother of the Minister responsible for the concept had happened to have bought some of the farms surrounding Stevenage shortly before the details of the intended New Town had been published.

North of Baldock the A1 continues as a dual carriageway until the junction with the A14 at Huntingdon.

After coming off the motorway, take the first left on a modern road layout signposted Willian. Head for the church in the centre of the village and the Fox is facing it. The Three Horseshoes on the way into the village is a cheerful locals' pub.

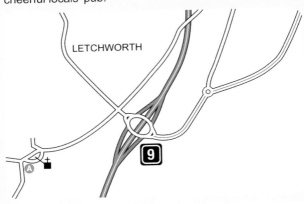

LETCHWORTH

The Fox at Willian

Baldock Lane, Willian, Herts.
01462 480 233
www.foxatwillian.co.uk
info@foxatwillian.co.uk

Satnav
SG6 2AE

Orders for food: Weekdays: Noon to 2.00pm and 6.30 pm to 9.15pm. Saturdays: Noon to 9.15pm. Sundays: Noon to 3.00pm.

££

A restaurant-cum-pub which has been refurbished so is now bare floors with wooden tables. Clean, bright and airy with a cheerful and friendly staff.

B **The George Brasserie**

High Street, Buckden, Cambs
01480 812 300
www.thegeorgebuckden.com
mail@thegeorgebuckden.com

Satnav
PE19 5XA

Orders for food: Daily: Noon to 2.30pm and 7.00pm to 9.30pm. Sundays: Noon to 3.00pm and 7.00pm to 9.00pm. Breakfast from 8am daily. Afternoon tea 3-5pm.

 £££

Originally a Georgian coaching inn, it is now a smart efficient brasserie which serves breakfasts, light lunches, teas and dinners. The bedrooms are all named after a George, such as Handel, Orwell or Shaw. There is outside seating in the courtyard for sunny days and a range of boutique shops in the building in case it is raining!

HUNTINGDON TO GRANTHAM

TO INCLUDE JUNCTIONS 13 TO 17

The first stretch, after crossing over the A14, is a four-lane motorway until Peterborough and then dual-carriageway to Grantham.

Stamford is a remarkable town for being in a time warp. It should be congratulated for turning down a government grant to have hanging baskets, daily street markets and no parking. The George Hotel in Stamford is world famous.

Grantham is now better known for being the birthplace of Margaret Thatcher.

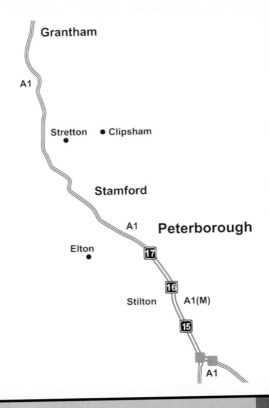

Coming from the north come off at the first junction and go straight on over the three roundabouts on the old A1 road marked Sawtry. At the fourth go left signed Woodwalton. At a T junction turn left marked Abbotts Ripon. When you cross over the railway you are almost there. For those coming from the south come off at the junction and at the first roundabout go left signed Woodwalton. It is worth the additional time to get to the Abbotts Elm.

Ⓐ The Abbots Elm

Main Road, Abbots Rippon, Cambs.
01487 773 773

Satnav
PE28 2PA

www.theabbotselm.co.uk
info@theabbotselm.co.uk

Orders for food: Monday to Saturday: Noon to 2.00pm and 7.00pm to 9.00pm. Sunday: Noon to 2.30pm.

££/£££

John and Julia Abbey took it over as a burnt out shell and rebuilt it as a spacious restaurant cum pub with modern comfort. The service is friendly and the menu is good. We arrived after last orders for food but John without a moments hesitation said that as a table was still ordering there was no problem. A delicious coq au vin appeared.

Take the B1043 south, and then almost immediately bear right to Stilton. Those looking for the home of Stilton Cheese could be disappointed, as it is actually made in Melton Mowbray. Nevertheless all five varieties of Stilton are served at the Bell Inn Hotel.

Places of interest
Peterborough Cathedral – 4 miles

A Bell Inn Hotel

Great North Road, Stilton, Cambs.
01733 241 066
www.thebellstilton.co.uk
reception@thebellstilton.co.uk
Orders for food: Monday to Saturday: Noon to 2.30pm and 6.00pm to 9.30pm. Sundays: Noon to 3.00pm and 6.00pm to 9pm.

Satnav
PE7 3RA

£££

A 16th-century coaching inn and now a privately owned well-furnished hotel with two bars, a bistro and a galleried restaurant on two levels under beamed ceilings. There is outside seating in an enclosed garden and courtyard, as well as private parking. Dick Turpin's room, where he rested between nefarious operations, is still in use as the resident's lounge.

A1(M) | **17** Peterborough, Wisbech (A1139) Northampton, Oundle A605

Take the A605 to Oundle. After 4 miles turn right signed Elton. The Loch Fyne Restaurant is 100 yards on the right in this rural village. The Black Bull is beyond Elton Hall, on the left.

Ⓐ **Loch Fyne Restaurant**

The Old Dairy, Elton, Northants
01832 280 298
www.lochfyneseafoodandgrill.co.uk
1687@greeneking.co.uk

Satnav
PE8 6SH

Orders for food: Mondays - Thursdays: 11.00am to 10.00pm. Fridays: 11.00am to 10.30pm. Saturdays: 9.00am to 10.30pm. Sundays: 9.00am to 10.00pm

£££

The menu and timings have changed but breakfasts are still available on Saturdays and Sundays. A comfortable restaurant where fresh fish and seafood dishes are a speciality. There is a set menu every day from 12.00am until 6.00pm offering two courses for £10.45.

B The Black Horse

Satnav
PE8 6RU

Overend, Elton, Northants
01832 281 222
www.theblackhorseelton.co.uk
info@theblackhorseelton.co.uk
Orders for food: Mondays to Saturdays: Noon to
2.30pm and 6.00pm to 9.30pm. Sundays: Noon to
3.30pm and 4.30pm to 8.00pm.

                                        ££

It has recently been taken over and renovated so is now
a friendly cheerful place with comfortable eating areas
and a bar. A large garden for summer evenings and a
car park opposite.

Access to Stamford off the A1 has been improved replacing the old simple roundabout. The William Cecil is on the right as you come into the town.

Places of interest
Burghley House (16th C) Pte - 1mile.

▲ The William Cecil at Stamford

Satnav
PE9 2LJ

St Martins, Stamford, Lincs.
01780 750 070
www. thewilliamcecil.co.uk
enquiries@thewilliamcecil.co.uk

Orders for food: Weekdays: Noon to 2.30pm and 6.30pm to 9.00pm. Saturday & Sundays: Noon to 2.30pm and 7.00pm to 9.30pm.
Breakfast: 7.00am to 9.30am.

££/£££

A must for the weary traveller as it has charm and character with a friendly welcome to put you at your ease. For those who have some spare time the restaurant has an excellent menu but the bar meals are equally good. After lunch you can walk in the grounds of Burghley House or else in Stamford itself which is the quintessence of an old English Market town.

For the Jackson Stops take the road to Stretton where it is signed from the road. The Olive Branch is in the next village of Clipsham on the left by a sharp bend.

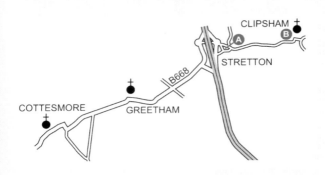

 Jackson Stops

Rookery Road, Stretton, Rutland
01780 410 237
www.thejacksonstops.com
info@thejacksonstops.com
Orders for food: Weekdays: Noon to 2.30pm and 6.30pm to 9.00pm. Sundays: Noon to 2.30pm. Mondays: Closed.

Satnav
LE15 7RA

££

A privately owned pub-cum-restaurant in an old building which has been divided into several small dining rooms. The menu is imaginative and the welcome friendly. You will have to ask why it is so called.

A1 Oakham B668
Stretton

ⓑ The Olive Branch
Main Street, Clipsham, Leics.
01780 410 355

Satnav
LE15 7SH

www.theolivebranchpub.com
info@theolivebranchpub.com

Orders for food: Monday to Thursdays: Noon to
2.00pm and 6.30pm to 9.30pm. Fridays, Saturdays and
Sundays: Noon to 3.00pm and 7.00pm to 9.30pm.

£££

A deservedly award-winning pub-cum-restaurant with
comfortable dining areas. Mellow brickwork, subdued
lighting and log fires give a cosy atmosphere. Excellent
food with local produce, including the famous
Lincolnshire sausages. A well-tended garden, so outside
dining in the evening.

GRANTHAM TO FERRYBRIDGE

TO INCLUDE JUNCTIONS 34 TO 38

This part has a short section of motorway near Doncaster but otherwise it is dual carriageway throughout. From Grantham, it is flat open countryside. At Newark, you will cross over the River Trent, the historical divide between North and South England.

The dual carriageway from Doncaster to Ferrybridge may now be upgraded to motorway standard, sooner rather than later.

The condensing towers of the Ferrybridge Power Station have been a familiar landmark for generations.

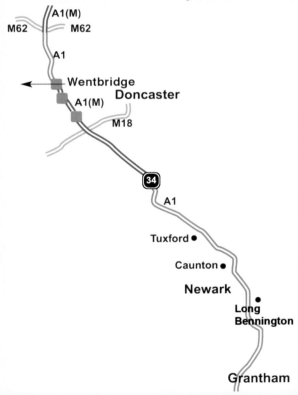

Long Bennington is on the old Great North Road but is now bypassed so it is a haven of peace from the noise

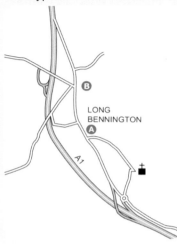

of traffic. It is still an attractive village as the new brick built houses are well designed and fit in sympathically with the old.

A Reindeer Inn

22 Main Road, Long Bennington, Nottinghamshire
01400 281 382
www.reindeerinn.co.uk
janet@reindeerinn.co.uk

Satnav
NG23 5EH

Orders for food: Mondays to Saturdays: Noon to 2.00pm and 6.30pm to 9.00pm. Sundays: Noon to 2.30pm

££

A friendly welcome in this family-owned inn, with a continental feel. Outside seating at the front of the house. Good atmosphere and a cheerful service coupled with a good menu.

B Royal Oak

Satnav
NG23 5DJ

Main Road, Long Bennington, Notts
01400 281 332

Orders for food: Noon to 2.00pm and 6.00pm to
9.00pm. Sundays: Noon to 2.30pm. Mondays: No
evening meals.

££

A friendly locals' pub with a comfortable dining area
under the auspices of Anthony Jacobs. Pleasant décor
and efficient service. A good menu but bar meals are
available. A garden at the rear for warm evenings.

North of Newark there is a sign saying Caunton which is easy to use from both directions. Caunton is 3 miles to the west on a narrow road through some uninteresting countryside. The level crossing on the main line could add minutes to your journey. In the middle of the village

is a turning to the left by what was probably the blacksmith. The Caunton Beck is on your left after a sharp bend.

Ⓐ Caunton Beck

Main Street, Caunton, Notts.
01636 636 793
www.wigandmitre.com
email@cauntonbeck.com

Satnav
NG23 6AB

Orders for food: Daily: 9.00am to 10.00pm. Sundays: 9.00am to 9.30pm. Breakfasts: 9.00am to 11.30am.

££

A brick-built range of buildings using old materials, it is now a comfortable restaurant with a bar. A cheerful atmosphere with a range of dining areas. Good wine list and traditional food with efficient and helpful service, especially after I had mislaid my mobile telephone.

A1

The roundabout has been updated and rebuilt. Take the B1164 to Tuxford, and the Mussel and Crab is 600 yards on the right.

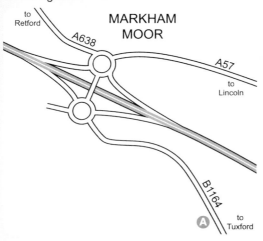

 Mussel and Crab

Satnav
NG22 0PJ

Sibthorpe Hill, Tuxford, Notts.
01777 870 491
www.musselandcrab.com
musselandcrab@hotmail.com

Orders for food: Monday to Saturday: 11.30am to 2.20pm and 6.00pm to 10.00pm. Sundays: Noon to 2.45pm and 6.00pm to 9.00pm.

£££

A privately owned country restaurant in a converted farmhouse. On entering you will be treated to the sound of the sea. There are several dining areas, in a modern style, and traditional bar meals can also be had. Al fresco also possible. Friendly, efficient service and excellent fish dishes.

Wentbridge is so named as it was the bridge over the River Went. Easy to reach from the A1 from both directions but it is at the bottom of a hill, so check the brakes.

Blue Bell Inn

Great North Road, Wentbridge, W. Yorksire
01977 620 697

Satnav
WF8 3JP

www.bluebellwentbridge.co.uk
info@bluebellwentbridge.co.uk

Orders for food: Daily: Noon to 2.30pm and 5.00pm to 9.00pm. Sundays: Noon to 7.00pm.

££

The original sign is still on view from the time the pub was renovated in 1633. It has since been updated and is now a comfortable, beamed and cheerful locals' pub with dining areas. The food is cooked to order so not instant. Two beer gardens outside.

FERRYBRIDGE TO SCOTCH CORNER

TO INCLUDE JUNCTIONS TO

This section has now been upgraded to motorway standard from Ferrybridge to Leeming. It was going to be upgraded from there north to Scotch Corner and this is now being done.

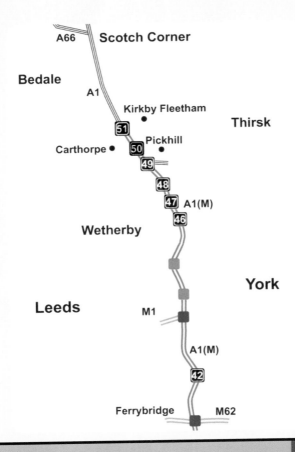

Since the upgrading of this section to a motorway,
it is easier to find the Chequers Inn form Junction 42.

Ⓐ Chequers Inn

Main Street, Ledsham, S.Yorks.
01977 683 135
www.chequersinn.com
c.j.wraith@btconnect.com

Satnav
LS25 5LP

Orders for food: Monday to Saturday: Noon to 9.15pm.
Sundays: Noon to 6.00pm.

 ££

 A Free House in the
middle of this estate
village. It was closed all
day on Sunday because
the lady of the manor in
1830 was abused on her
way to church by estate
workers pouring out of
the pub. It is however,
now open after the
Church service. Bar
meals downstairs and a comfortable restaurant above.
The menu includes steak pie and lamb sjanks which are
in demand.

This is really for those driving down from the north and looking for somewhere to stop before getting onto the M1 with its dearth of suitable places. The Arabian Horse is on the left in the village before the bridge. You then join the M1 at Junction 47.

 The Arabian Horse

Satnav
LS25 3AA

Main Street, Aberford, W.Yorks.
0113 281 3312
www.arabianhorsepublichouse.co.uk
info@arabianhorsepublichouse.co.uk

Orders for food: Mondays: 5.00pm to 8.00pm. Tuesdays to Thursdays: Noon to 2.00pm and 5.00pm to 8.00pm. Fridays and Saturdays: Noon to 2.00pm and 6.00pm to 9.00pm. Sundays: 12.30pm to 4.00pm. Breakfasts: Saturdays and Sundays: 9.00am to 11.00am.

 ££

Apparently the only pub to be so called as a result of the first Arab horses imported to the country being stranded in Aberford by bad weather.
A no frills village pub but comfortable with carpets and a large inglenook fire. My soup arrived within minutes of ordering and the service was cheerful.

For the Fox and Hounds turn right before Bickerton and then left at the T-junction in Walton. The pub is to the left on a sharp left-hand bend.

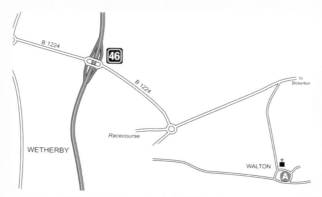

The Fox and Hounds

Satnav **LS23 7DQ**

Hall Park Road, Walton, W. Yorks.
01937 2 192
www.thefoxandhoundswalton.com
basil@thefoxandhoundswalton.com

Orders for food: Monday to Saturday: Noon to 2.00pm and 5.30pm to 9.00pm. Sundays: Noon to 3.00pm and 5.00pm to 7.00pm.

££

A thoroughly agreeable family run pub-cum-restaurant with friendly and efficient service. My crab soup with home-baked bread was good. Car park at rear, but take care coming out with a blind corner on the left, especially after such a good meal.

Take the A59 towards Knaresborough. After half a mile turn right to Coneythorpe. The Tiger is on your right as you come into the village.

Ⓐ **The Tiger**

Shortshill Lane, Coneythorpe, N.Yorks
01423 863 632
www.tiger-inn.co.uk

Orders for food: Noon to 9.00pm.
Sundays: Noon to 8.00pm.

Satnav
HG5 0RY

££

A deservedly popular place as it is family-owned and Victoria will make sure that you are given a cheerful Yorkshire welcome. The dining room at the rear is decorated with stags' heads, violins, fishing rods and walking sticks. My mussels were excellent and sensibly priced.

Ferrensby is on the A6055 to Knaresborough. For Roecliffe drive into the outskirts of Boroughbridge and take the road marked Roecliffe. Turn left at the roundabout.
For the Old Punch Bowl take the A168 south for two miles and turn left to Grafton. If going south rejoin at junction 47.

Places of interest
Newby Hall (17thC &18thC) HHA – 8 miles.
Roman city of Isurium.

Ⓐ The Crown Inn

Satnav
YO51 9LY

High Street, Roecliffe, N.Yorks.
01423 322 300
www.crowninnroecliffe.com
info@crowninnroecliffe.com

Orders for food: Noon to 2.15pm and 6.00pm to 9.00pm. Sundays: Noon to 7.00pm.

   £££

Originally a 16th-century inn, it was bought by Karl Mainey and he has made it into a friendly, comfortable and relaxed place to have a good meal. A restaurant to the left and a large bar area to the right of the front door. An enjoyable stop-over.

B General Tarleton

Satnav
HG5 0PZ

Boroughbridge Road, Ferrensby, N.Yorks.
01423 340 284
www.generaltarleton.co.uk
gti@generaltarleton.co.uk
Orders for food: Mondays to Thurs: Noon to 2.00pm and 5.30pm to 9.00pm. Fridays and Saturdays: Noon to 2.00pm and 5.30pm to 9.15pm. Sundays: Noon to 2.00pm and 5.30pm to 8.30pm.

££

A privately owned restaurant and hotel with contemporary furnished bedrooms. It is reputed to have the best cuisine in Yorkshire and gives a warm welcome from a young professional staff in a relaxed atmosphere. Children welcome.

C The Old Punch Bowl

Satnav
YO51 9QY

Main Road, Marton-cum-Grafton, Yorks
01423 322 519
www.thepunchbowlmartoncumgrafton.com
enquiries@thepunchbowlmartoncumgrafton.com

Orders for food: Daily: 12 Noon to 2.30pm and 5.30pm to 9.30pm. Sundays: Noon to 3.00pm and 5.30pm to 8.30pm.

£££

An old 17th Century ale house which has recently been stylishly modernised. It still has low beams and flagstone floors, polished tables and terracotta floors. In the winter there is a log fire and outside there is comfortable seating under the largest parasol/umbrella in Yorkshire. For racing car enthusiasts there is a designated room to Eddie Shine, who, in the 1950's and 60's, was a famous racing driver.

The junction is not directly affected by the upgrading to motorway standard of the A1 to Leeming. Turn off the road marked Asenby.

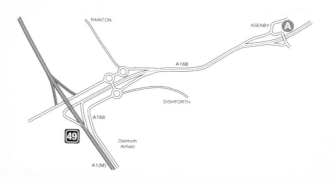

 The Crab and Lobster

Main Street, Asenby, Thirsk, N. Yorks.
01845 577 286

Satnav
YO7 3QL

www.crabandlobster.co.uk
reservations@crabandlobster.co.uk

Orders for food: Weekdays: Noon to 2.00pm and 7.00pm to 9.30pm. Saturdays: Noon to 2.00pm and 6.30pm to 9.00pm. Daily: A limited menu from 3.30pm to 5.00pm.

£££

A quirky restaurant with a bar. One of the more unusual places for a stop-over on a motorway! The décor has been done with imagination and the set menu (which obviously specialises in fish) is value for money. The Crab Manor Hotel is next door.

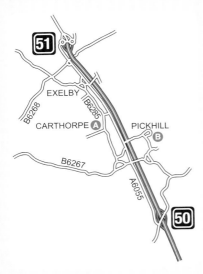

The Fox and Hounds, Nags Head and Green Dragon are between Junction 50 and 51 so take the A6065 (the old A1) from either end depending on direction of travel.

Ⓐ Fox and Hounds

Satnav
DL8 2LG

Main Street, Carthorpe, N.Yorks.
01845 567 433
www.foxandhoundscarthorpe.co.uk
info@foxandhoundscarthorpe.co.uk

Orders for food: Daily: Noon to 2.00pm and 7.00pm to 9.30pm. Sunday: Noon to 2.00pm and 7.00pm to 9.00pm. Closed Mondays.

££

Vince (who is an ex-Marine) and Helen Taylor run a cheerful pub-cum-restaurant serving high quality traditional fare in what was once the village smithy. The bellows and blacksmith's fire are still in evidence in the dining room.

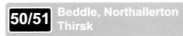

ⓑ Nags Head

Main Street, Pickhill, N.Yorks.
01845 567 391
www.nagsheadpickhill.co.uk
enquiries@nagsheadpickhill.co.uk

Satnav
YO7 4JG

Orders for food: Weekdays: Noon to 2.00pm and
6.00pm to 9.30pm. Sundays: Noon to 3.00pm and
5.30pm to 8.00pm. Breakfast available.

   ££/£££

It is really a comfortable inn,situated in an agricultural
village, with a separate dining room. However excellent
bar meals are also available for those in a hurry. Good
service and food.

The Black Horse Inn and Greyhound Inn are on the section of the A1 which is being rebuilt to motorway standard.

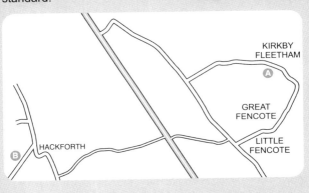

KIRKBY
FLEETHAM

Ⓐ

GREAT
FENCOTE

LITTLE
FENCOTE

Ⓑ HACKFORTH

Ⓐ Black Horse Inn

Satnav
DL7 0SH

Lumley Lane, Kirkby Fleetham, N.Yorks.
01609 749 010
www.blackhorsekirkbyfleetham.com
gm@blackhorsekirkbyfleetham.com

Orders for food: Monday to Thursday: Noon to 2.30pm and 5.00pm to 9.00pm. Friday and Saturday: Noon to 2.30pm and 5.00pm to 9.30pm.
Sunday: Noon to 7.00pm.

£££

A village pub which has recently been well renovated with a restaurant and a stone- flagged bar area. Classic dishes with hand-pulled ales and good wines. Friendly staff who have worked hard to make it a success.

❸ The Greyhound
Main Street, Hackforth. N.Yorks
01748 813 360

Satnav
DL8 1PB

www.greyhoundathackforth.co.uk

info@greyhoundathackforth.co.uk

Orders for food: Wednesday to Saturdays: Noon
to 2.30pm and 5.30pm to 9.00pm. Sundays: Noon
to 3.00pm. Mondays: no food served and no lunch
on Tuesdays.

 £

The Greyhound has had a chequered history over the
past ten years. It is privately owned and Mike Miles has
now taken it over. He gave me a friendly welcome even
after it had officially closed for food. There is a separate
dining room for those wanting more privacy Theakstons
and Black Sheep would appear to be the favourite brews.

SCOTCH CORNER
TO NEWCASTLE

JUNCTIONS 56 TO 65

Not the most inspiring countryside. Durham Cathedral to the west of the motorway is a World Heritage Site and is one of the most remarkable buildings in the country, known as "the loveliest building on Planet Earth".

The Angel of the North will greet you at the other end.

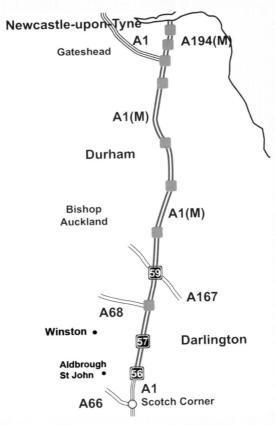

A1(M)

56 Piercebridge B6275
Barton, Darlington

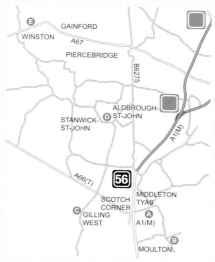

The building of the new motorway will cause disruption until 2017, so try your Sat nav.

Shoulder of Mutton

Satnav
DL10 6QX

Main Road, Middleton Tyas, N. Yorkshire
01325 377 271

www.shoulderofmuttonmiddletontyas.co.uk
shoulderofmutton1@live.co.uk

Orders for food: Mondays: 6.00pm to 9.00pm (closed for lunch). Tuesdays to Thursdays: Noon to 2.00pm and 6.00pm to 9.00pm. Fridays & Saturdays: Noon to 2.00pm and 6.00pm to 9.30pm. Sundays: Noon to 4.30pm and 5.30pm to 8.30pm.

££

A 300 year old pub serving cask ale with an imaginative menu. Cheerful welcome and a good atmosphere. Fran and Kevin Hacking have rejuvenated it and the cooking is back to its previous excellent standard. Children and dogs are welcome.

B The Black Bull

Satnav
DL10 6QJ

HigMain street, Moulton, N.Yorks
01325 377 556
enquiries@theblackbullmoulton.com
Orders for food: Monday-Saturday. Noon - 2.30pm and
5.30pm - 9.30pm. Sunday: Noon - 3.00pm and 5.30pm
- 8.30pm.

£££

Recently acquired by the
Provenance Inns Group, the
Black Bull has undergone a
transformation, with bright
décor, plenty of light and
wide open areas. There are
private dining rooms and the
emphasis is on fish. The
service is friendly and
efficient and some of the old
staff are still there.

C White Swan

Satnav
DL10 5JG

High Street, Gilling West, N.Yorks
01748 825 122
www.thewhiteswan.co
dh.dean@googlemail.com
Orders for food: Daily: Noon to 9.30pm.

££

An ideal stopover for
those driving on the A66
to or from Penrith and
Scotch Corner. A rural
village pub with a friendly
welcome and atmosphere.
Real ales and craft beers
and the food is from
known local suppliers.

We had an excellent light lunch before dashing on.

A1(M)   56   Piercebridge B6275 Barton, Darlington

ⓓ The Stanwick

Satnav
DL11 7SZ

High Green, Aldbrough St. John, N.Yorkshire
01325 374 258
www.thestanwickinn.co.uk
enquiries@thestanwick.co.uk

Orders for food: Mondays to Fridays: Noon to 2.00pm
and 5.30pm to 9.30pm. Saturdays: Noon to 2.00pm and
6.30pm to 9.30pm. Sundays: Noon to 5.00pm.

££

Since Neil and Helen
Maddison-Potts took it over it
has been going from strength
to strength as the food is
excellent. It is situated on the
village green so there is ample
scope for exercising the dogs
(or children) For the non
drivers there is a range of ales
including Daleside Bitter, Jarrow Rivet Catcher and
village brewed- Mithril Ale.

ⓔ Bridgewater Arms

Satnav
DL2 3RN

Main Street, Winston, Co. Durham
01325 730 302
www.thebridgewaterarms.com

Orders for food: Tuesdays to Saturdays: Noon to
2.00pm. 6.00pm to 9.00pm. Closed: Sundays and
Mondays.

££

Paul Grundy was at the
Black Bull in Moulton
before he took over the
tenancy so the food is
excellent and at a
reasonable price. It is a
converted school house
- hence the alphabet
decoration - but is well furnished, comfortable and
friendly. Well worth the additional mileage.

Do not bear left on the first roundabout but look out for
the Aycliffe sign. At the traffic lights turn right. After some
30 yards turn right at the corner and The County is 100
yards down on the left facing onto the green.

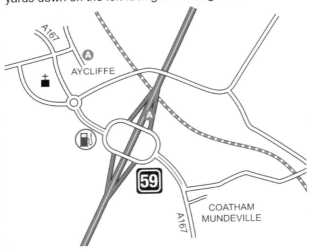

The County

Satnav
DL5 6LX

13 The Green, Aycliffe Village, Co. Durham
01325 312 273
www.thecountyaycliffevillage.com
info@thecountyaycliffevillage.com
Orders for food: Weekdays: Noon to 2.00pm and
5.30pm to 9.00pm. Sundays: Noon to 9.00pm.

££

A modernised country-style
pub on the village green. It
has changed hands and is
now carpeted throughout so
is less noisy. Tony Blair
brought President Chirac of
France to have dinner here.
Some outside eating. French
not essential.

A3(M)

A3(M) Horndean to Portsmouth

JUNCTIONS 1 TO 5

A short stretch of motorway, which was completed in 1979 to ease the traffic flow at the junction of the A3 to the M27.

South of Petersfield, the motorway climbs up to the high ground overlooking Portsmouth Harbour and the naval dockyards. HMS Victory is dry-docked there and the home of the Submarine Museum is over the harbour entrance at Gosport. Along the escarpment are a range of forts built by Palmerston in the 1860s to protect the coast against an expected invasion by the French.

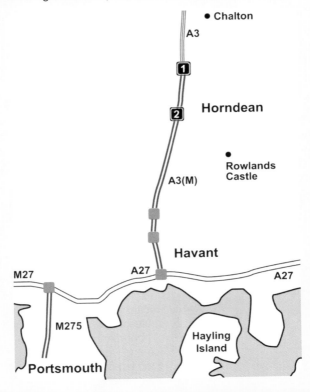

Driving south, the turnoff for Chalton is 2 miles from the start of the motorway section. Going north it is more complicated as you will have to take a left turning signed Clanfield, follow alongside the dual carriageway for half a mile and then cross over. To continue your journey, go over the A3 and drive on north for about a mile.

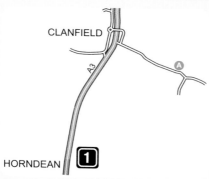

CLANFIELD

A3

Ⓐ

HORNDEAN **1**

Ⓐ **Red Lion**

Satnav
PO8 0BG

South Lane, Chalton, Hants.
02392 592 246
www.fullers.co.uk
redlion.chalton@fullers.co.uk

Orders for food: Mondays to Thursdays and Sundays: Noon to 9.00pm. Fridays and Saturdays: Noon to 9.30pm.

   ££

Apparently it was first licensed in 1503 and is Hampshire's oldest pub. It has, therefore, low beams, panelled walls and inglenook fires. It is furnished with traditional high-backed settles. There is a restaurant but bar meals are available. A friendly greeting and a good old-fashioned atmosphere.

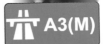
Come off at Junction 2. Carry on down the B2149 signed Westbourne. After the roundabout go through the woods and left to Rowlands Castle. There is another chance further on if you miss it.

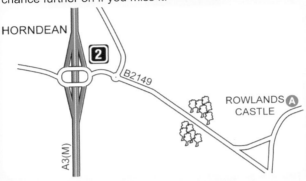

Places of interest
Stansted Park (1688-1903) HHA – 5 miles

Ⓐ **The Robin Hood Inn**

Satnav
PO9 6AB

The Green, Rowlands Castle, Hants.
02392 412 268
www.rowlandscastle.co.uk
robinhoodinn@hotmail.co.uk

Orders for food: Noon to 2.30pm and 6.00pm to 9.00pm.Sundays: Noon to 4.00pm

££

A restaurant with a bar, it is just within five minutes from the junction. A friendly atmosphere, light and airy, looking out over the village green.

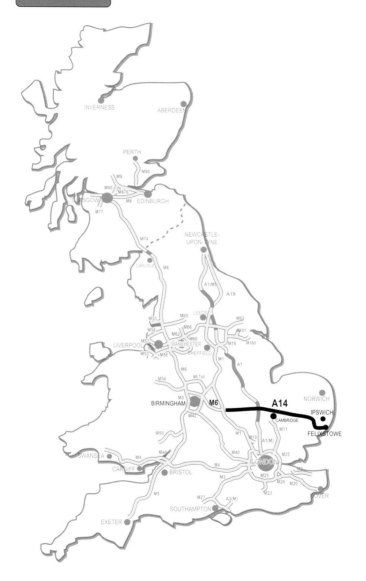

A14

JUNCTIONS 1 TO 60

This is a dual carriageway rather than a motorway but each of the junctions are numbered for easy recognition. It has become the main link between the Midlands to the port of Felixstowe and is therefore busy.

M1 TO HUNTINGDON

JUNCTIONS 1 TO 26

This section, which connects the M1 to the A1, passes through the attractive rolling countryside of the Shires.

Take the A508 south
through Maidwell and
Lamport is about 2.5 miles
further on.

Places of interest
Lamport Hall (17th-
18thC) HHA – 1mile

Kelmarsh Hall (1732)
HHA – 4 miles

Cottesbrooke Hall and
Gardens (1702) HHA –
6 miles

A The Swan

Harborough Road, Lamport, Northants.
01604 686 555
www.theswanatlamport.co.uk
theswanlamport@mcmanuspub.co.uk

Satnav
NN6 9EZ

Orders for food: Monday to Saturday: Noon to 9.00pm.
Sundays: Noon to 6.00pm.

££

One of the new
generation of restaurants
with bar areas. Now
owned by McManus
Taverns it has been
upgraded with modern
décor and open spaces.
It is efficient, with
courteous service.
A good view of the
countryside.

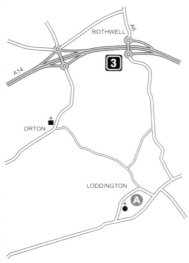

Take the road marked Orton Village Only. Turn left just before you get into Orton. After one mile, in Loddington turn right at the T junction and head for the church spire. The Hare is on the left.

Ⓐ The Hare
Main Street, Loddington, Northants.
01536 710 337
www.thehareatloddington.com
info@thehareloddington.com

Satnav
NN14 1LA

Orders for food: Weekdays: Noon to 2.00pm and 6.00pm to 9.30pm. Saturdays: Noon to 9.30pm. Sundays: Noon to 8.00pm.

££

A privately owned inn which has a reputation for good food. For those in a hurry, however there are bar meals and sandwiches. Outside seating at the front. It is advisable to book in advance.

No problems with the junction. Go straight on at the first roundabout going north. After the second road to the right keep a lookout for the road into Lowick – which is sharper than that shown on the plan.

Places of interest
Lyveden New Bield (1595) NT – 7 miles

Ⓐ The Snooty Fox

Satnav
NN14 3BH

Main Street, Lowick, Northants.
01832 733 434
www.thesnootyfoxlowick.com
info@thesnootyfoxlowick.com

Orders for food: Tuesday- Saturday: Noon to 2.00pm and 6.00pm to 9.00pm. Sundays: Noon to 3.00pm and 6.00pm to 9.00pm.   Mondays: Closed.

££

An upmarket pub-cum-restaurant in a range of old houses, one being the old Manor House. It has been converted into a comfortable and well-furnished hostelry with original carved beams and a dining area near the bar. It is noted for its cooking. A garden in front for summer days.

For Keyston head south on the B663 towards Raunds.
Zigzag through Keyston with the church on your right.
At the end of the village turn right and The Pheasant is
100 yards on the left.

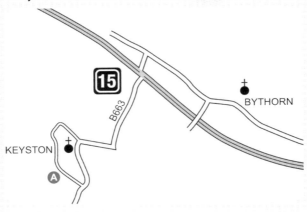

The Pheasant

Satnav
PE28 0RE

Loop Road, Keyston, Cambs.
01832 710 241
www.thepheasant-lowick.co.uk
info@thepheasant-lowick.co.uk

Orders for food: Tuesday to Saturday: Noon to 2.00pm
and 6.30pm to 9.30pm. Sundays: Noon to 3.30pm.
Mondays: Closed.

£££

Converted from a group of
thatched cottages in this
peaceful hamlet, it has been
comfortably furnished with a
lounge bar and three dining
areas. A good menu and
friendly service under the
auspices of Gerda and Simon.
A car park at the rear. Outside
seating in front as well as in
the garden.

HUNTINGDON TO BURY ST. EDMUNDS

JUNCTIONS **22** TO **42**

This section passes Huntingdon, Cambridge, Newmarket and Bury St. Edmunds. It is a busy section, full of lorries and speed traps, especially where it joins the M11

Cambridge needs no introduction and should be visited even though car parking is a problem.

Newmarket is famous the world over for horses and has a whiff of wealth and wellbeing.

Going further east, the countryside changes to a more rural atmosphere with small villages and an air of timelessness.

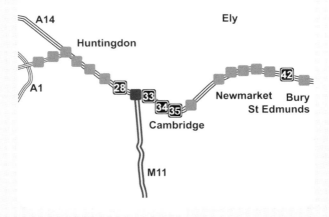

It is a long way from junction 28 but you will get into a muddle if you try coming off at J27 or 27A. Best switch on your satnav!

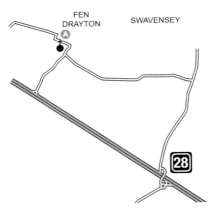

 The Three Tuns

Satnav
CB24 4SJ

High Street, Fen Drayton, Cambs.
01954 230 242
www.the3tuns.co.uk
info@the3tuns.co.uk

Orders for food: Monday to Friday: Noon to 2.00pm and 6.00pm to 9.00pm. Saturdays: Noon to 2.00pm and 6.00pm to 9.30pm. Sundays: Noon to 2.00pm.

   ££

A charming family-run pub, with Samantha taking the orders, her brother in the kitchen and her mother manning the bar. It was once the medieval Guildhall of the village so has a good atmosphere. The menu is wide-ranging but lighter fare can be had for those in a hurry, such as the leek, courgette and rosemary soup. There is a childrens' playground in the large garden and a smoking area.

Junction 34 for Horningsea is for the benefit of those driving east and then deciding to return westwards. However, help is at hand with Junction 33 as you can use that to go in the required direction.

Ⓐ **Crown & Punchbowl**

Satnav
CB25 9JG

High Street, Horningsea, Cambs.
01223 860 643
www.thecrownandpunchbowl.com
info@thecrownandpunchbowl.com
Orders for food: Monday to Thursday: Noon to 3.00pm and 6.30pm to 9.00pm. Friday to Saturday: Noon to 3.00pm and 6.30pm to 9.30pm. Sundays: Noon to 3.00pm.

££

An old pub which has been given a modern makeover of wooden floors, farmhouse tables and chairs, and soft lighting. The low beams and inglenook fire remain as does the friendly service by the helpful staff. There is no bar as such but the food is excellent, specialising in a variety of steak and fish. The bedrooms are clean and modern.

Take the A1303 towards Newmarket. After a mile turn
right where signed Little Wilbraham and continue
through the village. The Hole in the Wall is after a farm
on the right.

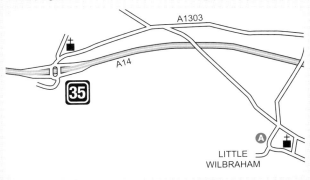

The Hole in the Wall

Satnav
CB21 5JY

2 High Street, Little Wilbraham, Cambs.
01223 812 282
www.holeinthewallcambrdige.com
enquiries@holeinthewallcambridge.co.uk
Orders for food: Monday to Saturdays: Noon to 2.00pm
(except Tuesdays) and 7.00pm to 9.00pm.
Sundays: Noon to 2.00pm. Closed Mondays.

££

A Free House in an old
cottage which has been an
Ale House since the 16th
century. It is now a
comfortable, low- beamed
hostelry with two separate
dining rooms serving delicious
food (to quote from one of our
readers). The kitchen and one
of the dining rooms is in a

more modern extension and there is an annex forming
an L shaped area for outside seating.

Head south from the junction marked Westley. At the first crossroads continue to Horringer. At the end of this village take a left and then first right at a crossroads. After a mile bear left at a Y junction to Whepstead. Bear right at Y junction with a sign - White Horse. To return take the road marked Chevington until you come to the A143, 2 miles south of Horringer.

Places of interest
Ickworth House (1795)
NT - 3 miles.

Ⓐ White Horse

Satnav
IP29 4SS

Rede Road, Whepstead, Suffolk
01284 735 760
www.whitehorsewhepstead.co.uk
d.i@whitehorsewhepstead.co.uk

Orders for food: Weekdays: Noon to 2.00pm and 7.00pm to 9.30pm. Sundays: Noon to 2.00pm.

£££

Garry and Di Kingshott have moved from the Beehive in Horringer and this old building has been renovated to make a traditional inn with comfort and good service. The home-made sausages are a speciality. Well-behaved children are welcome and dog owners will be glad to hear that Di has received an award from the local vet.

BURY ST EDMUNDS TO FELIXSTOWE

JUNCTIONS **43** TO **60**

Bury St Edmunds was once the capital of East Anglia.

St Edmund, the martyred King is buried in St Edmundsbury Cathedral which still dominates the old town. Apparently he had been the patron saint of England until St George took over in more militant times. It is said that in 1214 various barons met at St Edmund's Altar and swore an oath that they would force King John to sign the Magna Carta.

East of Bury St Edmunds the countryside becomes increasingly more rural with thatched and plastered cottages.

Ipswich is a traditional county town with a small port and some interesting houses.

From there the A14 follows the line of the River Orwell to the busy international port of Felixstowe and the reason for so many lorries.

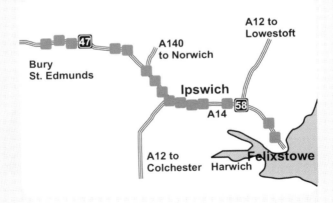

Take the A1088 to Norton and the Dog is on the right as you come into the village.

ⓐ The Norton Dog
Ixworth Road, Norton, Suffolk
01359 230 440
www.thenortondog.com
info@thenortondog.com

Satnav
IP31 3LP

Orders for food: Monday to Friday: Noon to 9.30pm. Saturdays: Noon to 10.00pm. Sundays: Noon to 9.00pm. Breakfast: 8.00am to 10.30am.

                                              £

A 16th-century village pub. The dining areas are of bare brick walls and low beams. Fresh locally grown produce with a gluten-free menu is on offer. Relax by an open fire, a sofa or in the garden.

The Ship is signposted from the main road. At Levington bear left and pass the church.

 LEVINGTON

The Ship Inn

Satnav
IP10 0LQ

Church Lane, Levington, Suffolk
01473 659 573
www.theshipinnlevington.co.uk
Orders for food: Daily: Noon to 2.30pm and 6.00pm to 8.30pm.
Saturdays: Noon to 8.30pm.
Sundays: Noon to 5.00pm.

££

The Ship Inn is an attractive, part-thatched traditional pub offering a warm welcome, good beer and food. Well behaved dogs are welcome in the bar and on the outdoor terrace.

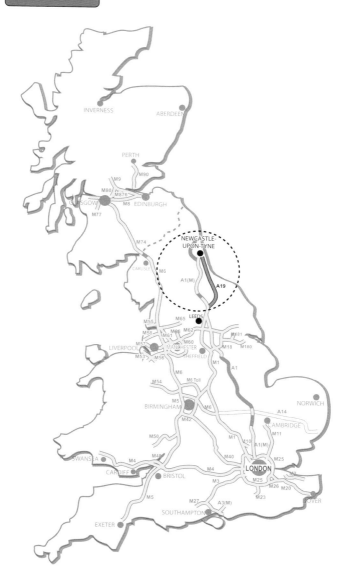

A19

THIRSK TO TYNE TUNNEL  A19

The upgrading to motorway standard of the A1 from
Bedale to Scotch Corner is due to be completed by 2017.
We therefore decided to include the A19 in the guide
which will bypass any likely hold-ups.

Although the exits are not numbered, it is a dual
carriageway throughout and much used when travelling
to or from Northumberland.

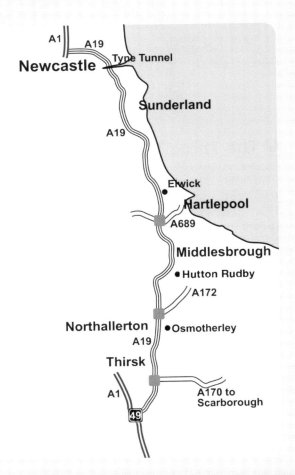

The A684 from Northallerton joins the A19 here. Osmotherley is on a minor road continuation of it. The village is attractive and is the starting point for many of the walkers trekking over the North Yorkshire Moors.

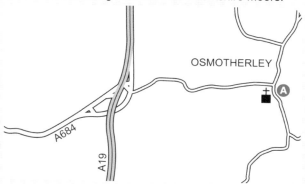

The Three Tuns

Satnav
DL6 3BD

South End, Osmotherley, N.Yorks.
01609 883 301
www.threetunsrestaurant.co.uk
enquiries@threetunsrestaurant.co.uk

Orders for food: Weekdays: Noon to 2.30pm and 5.30pm to 9.30pm. Sundays: Noon to 6.00pm.

      ££

A family-owned and run restaurant in this picturesque village in the North Yorkshire Moors. A well deserved reputation for high quality food in the Rennie Mackintosh inspired dining room. On warm days which we are told will be more often you can relax in the colourful garden. The bedrooms are comfortable for those wanting to spend longer in this part of the country.

Hutton Rudby is halfway between Middlesbrough and Thirsk. It is signed off the A19 and is about 2 miles distant. It is an attractive village on the banks of the

River Leven on the northern edge of the Cleveland Hills, so easy access to the North Yorkshire Moors.

🅐 The Bay Horse

Satnav
TS15 0DA

Northside, Hutton Rudby, N.Yorks.
01642 700 252
www.the-bay-horse.co.uk
jill.bayhorse@btinternet.com
Orders for food: Weekdays: Noon to 2.00pm and 6.00pm to 9.30pm. Sundays: Noon to 2.30pm. Mondays: No meals.

££

A family-owned and run locals' pub which has changed hands. It is some 300 years old, so is oak-beamed with Yorkshire windows. An added attraction is the large garden for summer use or for getting one's breath back after a long walk.

An easy junction even though you may have to cross over the dual carriageway. Elwick is attractive with a large green like many northern villages. The Mcorville Inn is next door as an alternative.

Spotted Cow Inn

31 The Green, Elwick, Cleveland
01429 266 373
spottedcow.elwick@email.com
Orders for food: Daily: Noon to 9.00pm.

Satnav
TS27 3EF

£

A locals' pub in this attractive village. Dining areas dominated by a large bar but with a cheerful atmosphere. No dogs in the eating areas but children welcome.

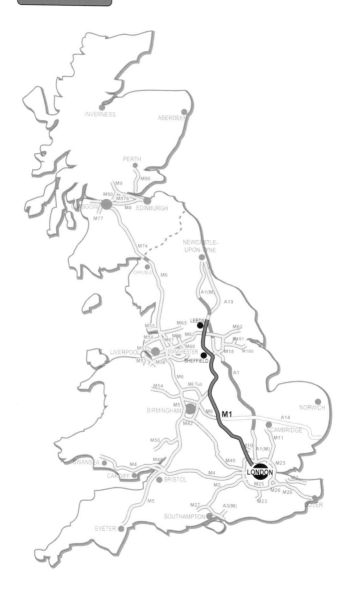

M1

JUNCTIONS 8 TO 48

The M1 was the first major motorway to be built in the U.K. The first section of 72 miles was built by Messrs. Laing & Son at a cost of £50 million and was completed in 19 months. It was opened in November 1959 by the then Minister of Transport, Ernest Marples, who in real life was a director of a building contracting firm. In 1965 a 70mph speed limit was imposed after it was being used as a test track by an AC Cobra Le Mans car doing 183mph at 4am one wintry morning. The final link of the M1, from Leeds to the A1(M), of about 9 miles, was completed in 1999 at a cost of £140 million.

HEMEL HEMPSTEAD TO CRICK

JUNCTIONS 8 TO 18

A congested section of the motorway until past the junction with the M6.

The junction has now been upgraded and rebuilt so is therefore more confusing. However Harlington is still clearly signed. In the village turn right at the T junction by the green. For the French Horn follow the map!

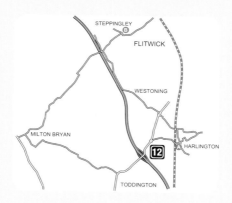

Ⓐ The Carpenters Arms

Satnav
LU5 6LS

Sundon Road, Harlington, Beds.
01525 872 384

Orders for food: Mondays to Fridays: Noon to 2.00pm and 6.00pm to 9.00pm. Fridays and Saturdays: Noon to 9.00pm. Sundays: Noon to 4.00pm

££

A tenanted pub of Enterprise Inns which Terry Payne has recently taken over. Low beams and a cheerful atmosphere make it an agreable stop over for the passing motorist. A beer garden at the back and the village green opposite for warmer days.

ⓑ The French Horn

Satnav
MK45 5AU

Church End, Steppingley, Beds.
01525 720 122
www.thefrenchhornpub.com
info@thefrenchhornpub.com

Orders for food: Weekdays: Noon to 3.00pm and
6.00pm to 10.00pm. Saturdays: Noon to 10.00pm.
Sundays: Noon to 9.00pm.

Originally a late 18th-century farmhouse it has been
converted to give a warm welcome by the owners, into
an old-world atmosphere of flagstoned floors, leather
chairs and wooden tables. There is a spacious dining
room but it can get busy at peak periods, so it is
advisable to book.

Nothing much to explain, as it is very straightforward.

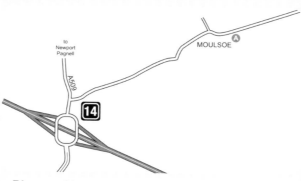

Places of interest
Bletchley Park (Pte) – 6 miles

Carrington Arms

Cranfield Road, Moulsoe, Bucks.
01908 218 050
www.thecarringtonarms.co.uk
enquries@thecarringtonarms.co.uk

Satnav
MK16 0HB

Orders for food: Daily: Noon to 10.00pm.
Breakfasts: Weekdays: 7.30am to 9.30am.
Weekends and Bank Holidays: 8.00am to Noon.

£££

A family run traditional
English Inn. Guests
choose from a
selection of local
Bedfordshire beef
prime cuts cooked to
their instruction on the
charcoal grill and
served by attentive
staff. An à la carte is
also available. The Bar
Menu offers lighter
options and pub favourites.

From the junction take the A45 to Flore. After less than
a mile turn left to Nether Heyford to get to the Olde Sun.
For the Bliss Tearoom turn left, as you enter Flore and
down a narrow residential road - but it is signed. The
White Hart is on the left in the village.

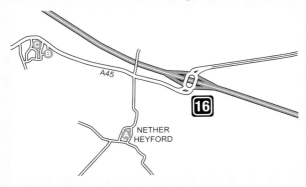

Ⓐ Olde Sun

Satnav
NN7 3LL

Middle Street, Nether Heyford, Northants.
01327 340 164

Orders for food: Monday to Thursday: Noon to 2.00pm
and 6.30pm to 9.00pm. Fridays & Saturdays: Noon to
2.30pm and 6.30pm to 9.00pm.
Sundays: Noon to 4.00pm.

£

A traditional old 18th-century pub with a warm
welcome. An eclectic mix of brass bric-a-brac to keep

visitors
occupied.
Bar meals
from two bar
areas
available for
lunch, but the
restaurant is
open in the
evenings.

ⓑ The Bliss Tearoom

Satnav
NN7 4LJ

Bliss Lane, Flore, Northants.
01327 342 283
www.blisslanenursery.co.uk/tearoom
geoflittlewood@hotmail.com

Orders for food: Mondays to Saturdays: 10.00am to 5.00pm. Sundays:10.00am to 4.00pm.
Winter: November to April: Daily: 10.00am to 4.00pm
Closed Tuesdays for baking.

£

A family run enterprise
where Geof Littlewood runs
the Tearoom and Farm Shop
and Chris his wife looks
after the Nursery of plants
which she has done for 35
years. The Tearoom serves
breakfasts, light lunches and
cream teas, all freshly prepared on the premises.

ⓒ The White Hart

Satnav
DL8 2HA

High Street, Flore, Northants.
01327 341 748
www.whitehartflore.co.uk
info@whitehartflore.co.uk

Orders for food: Tuesday to Friday: Noon to 2.30pm and 6.00pm to 9.00pm. Saturdays: Noon to 3.00pm and 6.00pm to 9.30pm. Sundays: Noon to 5.00pm. No meals on Mondays.

££

It has recently been
refurbished with timber or
flagged floors, comfortable
chairs and polished tables.
As a result it has gained an
enviable local reputation as
a place to dine and relax.

To get to The Moorings, (which was previously called Edwards), go straight on at the first roundabout and on again at the next one, over the canal and it is on the banks of the canal to the right. For Crick, take the A428 to the east and turn right at the first roundabout and left at the next. In Crick the Red Lion is on the right.

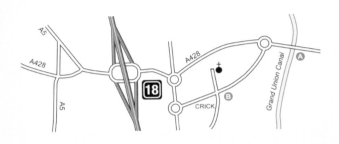

Ⓐ The Moorings

Satnav
NN6 7SQ

West Haddon Road, Crick, Northants.
01788 822 517
www.themooringscrick.co.uk
themooringscrick@yahoo.co.uk

Orders for food: Daily: 11.00am to 9.30pm
(in summer). Noon to 2.30pm and 6.30pm to 9.30pm
(in winter). Sundays: 11.00am to 5.00pm.

££

A privately owned restaurant by the canal. Simple home cooking with fresh produce and served with the minimum of fuss. Dogs may appreciate a walk along the canal bank.

Ⓑ The Red Lion

Satnav
NN6 7TX

Main Street, Crick, Northants.
01788 822 342
ptmarks180@tiscali.co.uk

Orders for food: Daily: Noon to 2.00pm and 6.30pm to 9.00pm. Sundays: Noon to 2.00pm.

££

It has been a coaching inn since the early 1700s and is still family-run with a dining area. It has low beams, as tall visitors will discover. Some outside seating and a car park at the rear. A congenial place where they pride themselves on their homemade steak pie with real ales.

RUGBY TO CHESTERFIELD

JUNCTIONS 19 TO 29

This seems to be a culinary desert, but there are some places worthy of a stopover.

There are however, some interesting places on which to feast the eye just off the motorway, such as Stanford Hall, Newstead Abbey, Hardwick Hall, Bolsover Castle and further afield Haddon Hall and Chatsworth.

Work started in January 2014 on building a motorway interchange at Junction 19 to give a direct link between the M6 and A14 which will affect local access as from September 2015.

For those driving south follow the signs marked A14 Felixstowe. Turn left at the first roundabout to Swinford for the Chequers or continue round for the Manor Farm Shop. You then have to work out how to continue south. For those coming from the south the same will apply in reverse order. From September 2015 this junction will be closed for local access.

Places of interest
Stanford Hall HHA – 2 miles

Ⓐ The Chequers

High Street, Swinford, Leics.
01788 860 318
www.chequersswinford.co.uk
chequersswinford@aol.com

Satnav
LE17 6BL

Orders for food: Daily: Noon to 2.00pm and 6.00pm to 9.00pm. Sundays: Noon to 3.00pm. No evening meals. Mondays: Closed for meals

£

A traditional friendly village pub with pub games and gas log fires. Meals are served in the bar with real ales or in the dining area. Garden and a playground.

Ⓑ Manor Farm Shop

Main Street, Catthorpe, Leics.
01788 869 002
www.manorfarmcatthorpe.co.uk
enquiries@manorfarmcatthorpe.co.uk

Satnav
LE17 6DB

Orders for food: Monday to Saturday: 9.00am to
4.00pm. Sundays: 10.00am to 4.00pm.

£

A genuine working farm which has diversified. In a
converted barn there is a Farm Shop selling a wide
range of local produce; a gift shop for kitchen
accessories, books, toys and cards and the Tea Room
which serves morning coffee, light lunches and
afternoon teas. There is outside seating and a car park.
Dogs on leads and children are welcome.

Lutterworth is a charming old market town and well
worth visiting. The Greyhound is on the left in the centre
of the town.

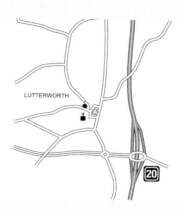

LUTTERWORTH

20

Ⓐ Greyhound Inn

Satnav
LE17 4BP

Market Street, Lutterworth, Leics.
01455 553 307
www.greyhoundinn.co.uk
bookings@greyhoundinn.co.uk

Orders for food: Weekdays: Noon to 2.00pm and
7.00pm to 9.30pm. Sunday: 12.30pm to 2.30pm and
7.00pm to 8.45pm.

£££

It was once an important Coaching
Inn on the Old Great North Road
and it is still an hospitable place
redolent of a bygone age with a
varied collection of clocks with
varied times. Nevertheless it gives a
warm welcome and a friendly
service. The old yard at the back is
now full of topiary and seats where
you sit on warm evenings and the
bedrooms are located around.

It is brown signed from the motorway. Take the A6 through Kegworth. At the end of the dual carriageway in Zouch look out for the B5324 to Ashby de la Zouch. After half a mile turn right to Long Whatton. The Falcon is on the south side of the road.

 The Falcon Inn

Main Street, Long Whatton, Leics. .
01509 842 416
www.thefalconinnlongwhatton.com
jed.otaki@yemail.com

Satnav
LE12 5DG

Orders for food: Daily: Noon to 2.00pm and 7.00pm to 9.00pm. Sundays: Noon to 4.00pm.

£££

A privately owned hotel cum pub. There is a garden at the rear equipped with patio heaters or umbrellas depending on the vagaries of the weather. The bedrooms are in a courtyard annex so easy for wheelchair users. It has an imaginative menu with an overtone of the Lebanon.

The junction is studded with the brown signs of the Tourist Board to all the great houses in the vicinity. Take the A6175 to Clay Cross. The sign to Heath to the right is not easy to see. For the Hardwick Inn take the small road to the left and continue until you go under the motorway and bear left for the Hardwick Inn and Hardwick Hall.

Places of interest
Hardwick Hall (c 1597) NT – 2 miles
Bolsover Castle (c1620) EH – 1 mile
Chatsworth (c1552-1820) – 18 miles
Sutton Scarsdale (c1720) – 1 mile
Haddon Hall (c1380 to 17thC) – 17 miles

Ⓐ Elm Tree

Mansfield Road, Heath, Derbys.
01246 850 490
www.theelmtreeheath.co.uk
info@theelmtreeheath.co.uk

Satnav
S44 5SE

Orders for food: Weekdays: Noon to 2.00pm and 6.00pm to 9.00pm. Fridays & Saturdays: Noon to 9.00pm. Sundays: Noon to 8.00pm.

££

A restaurant with a bar that featured in a previous edition. It is now refurbished with more space. The soup, served with home made bread and vegetables from their own garden, was particularly good.

M1

❶ The Hardwick Inn

Hardwick Park, Derbys.
01246 850 245
www.hardwickinn.co.uk
hardwickinn@hotmail.co.uk

Satnav
S44 5QJ

Orders for food: Monday to Saturday: 11.30am. to
9.30pm. Sundays: Noon to 9.00pm.

££

Built in the 16th century it has been converted into a
popular family owned Inn with several dining rooms,
friendly service and a busy but comfortable ambiance.
There is plenty of outside seating. It could become
crowded during the summer. Dogs welcome inside.

CHESTERFIELD TO A1(M)

JUNCTIONS **30** TO **48**

Here again there seem to be few, if any, worthwhile places to stop and rest. In fact there are none! This is a pity as at this stage of the journey you will be looking for just such a stopover.

There are places to see on the way however who have a restaurant or a tearoom. These include the Cannon Hall Museum on Junction 37 and Temple Newsam House (the Hampton Court of the North) by Junction 46.

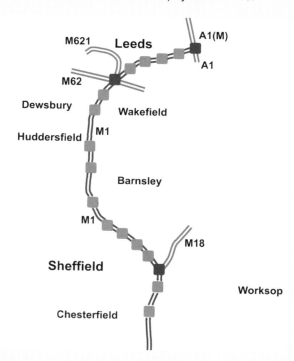

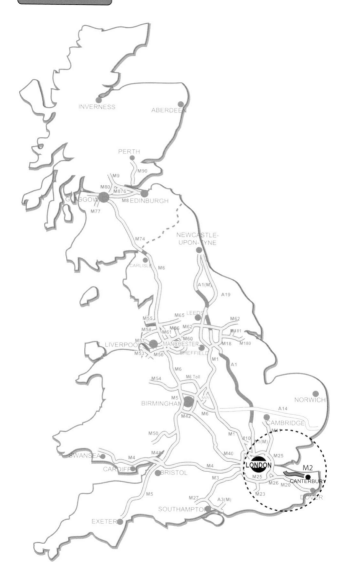

LONDON TO DOVER

  M2

JUNCTIONS 1 TO 7

One of the shorter motorways being only 25 miles in length but one of the first to be built in 1963.

It was designed to create a faster journey between London and the Channel Ports linking up with existing roads. The approach to London however remained abysmal. The connecting road from the Blackwall Tunnel and Greenwich and the link with the M25 has been much improved.

The traffic density was reduced after the construction of the M20 to the south and you can interchange easily between the two should the conditions become unbearable.

The motorway passes some historic towns such as Rochester, the setting for *Pickwick Papers* by Charles Dickens; the old Naval Dockyards at Chatham which were burnt by the Dutch in 1667; the ancient city of Canterbury, settled by the Romans and where Saint Augustine introduced Christianity to the country in AD 597 and where Thomas a Becket was murdered in the cathedral in 1173.

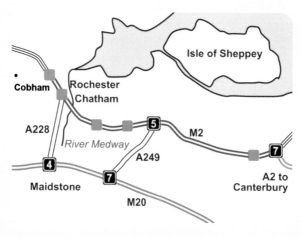

Take the A249 towards Maidstone and turn left signed
Oad Street. Up a hill on a narrow road. The centre is on
the left.

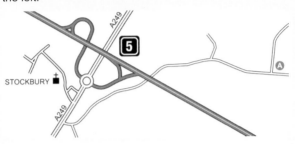

Places of interest
Stockbury features in the Domesday Book in 1086 as
Stochinberge.

B **Oad Street Centre**

Satnav
ME9 8LB

Oad Street, Nr Borden, Kent
01795 842 244
www.oadstreetcentre.co.uk
info@oadstreetcentre.co.uk

Orders for food: Daily: 9.30am to 5.30pm.
Breakfast from 9.30am.

££

The restaurant/
tearoom forms
part of a complex
of arts and crafts
workshops and
galleries so ideal
for those who
need to buy a
present. Morning
coffee and the Kentish cream teas are a firm favourite
to supplement a range of home baked cakes, scones
and biscuits. It is a refreshing change from the norm
for a quiet meal, a light luncheon or even a baguette.
There is also a childrens' menu if required.

Continue on the A299 towards Whitstable. After half a mile it is signed Faversham, Staplestreet and Hernhill. After Staplestreet turn left to Hernhill. The Red Lion is on the crossroads in the centre of the village opposite the church.

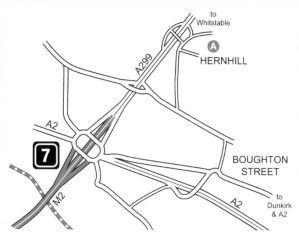

 Red Lion

The Green, Hernhill, Kent
01227 751 207
www.theredlion.org
enquries@theredlion.org

Satnav
ME13 9JR

Orders for food: Monday to Saturday: Noon to 2.30pm and 6.00pm to 9.00pm. Sundays: Noon to 8.00pm.

££

A privately owned half-timbered 14th-century house which has been converted into a pub and a restaurant with a Champagne bar upstairs under a medieval Crown Post and beamed roof. A garden for summer seating and a sundial dating from 1364 to speed you on your way.

JUNCTIONS 1 TO 12

This motorway connects London with the port at Southampton and with the south west of England by way of the A303.

The building of the continuation of the motorway past Winchester in 1994 meant the cutting of a trench at Twyford Down. This caused massive unrest by protestors and increased subsequent cost. It might have been cheaper to build a tunnel. The motorway passes Basingstoke, a new town which has managed to destroy any vestige of what had once been a pleasant market town. Winchester retains its historic atmosphere and is therefore full of visitors.

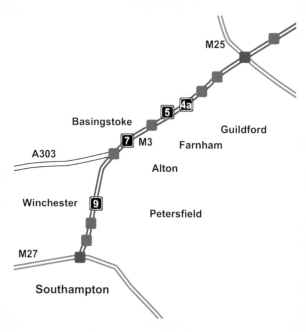

A simple junction and the pub is easy to find.

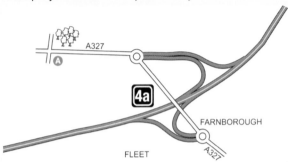

Places of interest
Napoleon III's Mausoleum, Farnborough – 3 miles
Airborne Forces Museum, Aldershot – 4 miles

 Crown and Cushion   Satnav
GU17 9UA

Minley Road, Blackwater, Surrey.
01252 545 253
www.baronspubs.com
manager.crownandcushion@baronspubs.com
Orders for food: Monday to Saturday: Noon to 9.30pm.
Sundays: Noon to 9.00pm.

££

An attractive rural pub in a wooded area. Log fires in the winter and sunny patios in the summer. Bar meals and traditional pub favorites as well as a childrens menu. It is said to be haunted by the mistress of Captain Blood whi tried to steal the Crown Jewels in 1671.

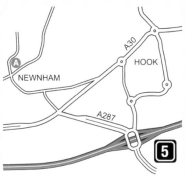

For the Old House take the A287 to the A30 and cross over the junction to Newham. The Old House is on the far side of the green. To get to the Mill House drive south on the A287 and at the first roundabout take the road to Odiham. The Mill House is on your right.

Places of interest
Old Basing House,
Hants C.C. - 5 miles

Ⓐ Old House at Home

Satnav
RG27 9AH

The Green, Newham, Hants.
01256 762 222
www.oldhousenewnham.co.uk
sukicblofeld@aol.com

Orders for food: Monday to Friday: Noon to 2.30pm and 6.00pm to 9.00pm. Saturdays: Noon to 3.00pm and 6.00pm to 9.00pm. Sundays: Noon to 3.00pm.

££

A country pub-cum-restaurant on the edge of the green. Outside seating in front and more in the garden behind. An attentive welcome and an imaginative menu. Suki and Olly Williams have been the owners for the past 11 years and run it with style and panache. Dogs outside and well-behaved children inside.

Mill House

Satnav
RG29 1ET

Hook Road, North Wanborough, Hants.
01256 702 953
www.millhouse-book.co.uk
mill.house@brunningandprice.co.uk

Orders for food: Daily: Noon to 10.00pm.
Sundays: Noon to 9.30pm.

££

This was in earlier editions but then changed hands. A
Grade II listed watermill with a lake and grounds. The
interior is beamed, a part of it being well cushioned
against impact. Friendly service even though we arrived
late but no problems with giving us lunch.

Not that difficult a junction - just follow the signs.

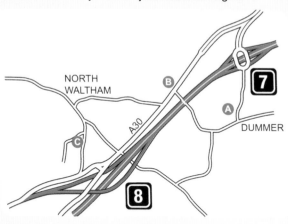

Places of interest
The Grange (18thC) EH – 8 miles

Ⓐ Queen Inn

Down Street, Dummer, Hants.
01256 397 367
www.thequeendummer.com
richardmoore49@btinternet.com

Satnav
RG25 2AD

Orders for food: Daily: Noon to 2.30pm and 6.30pm to 9.30pm. Sundays: Noon to 2.30pm and 7.00pm to 9.00pm.

££

A popular and well-known family-owned pub. It gets its name from the fourth wife of Henry VIII who was Anne of Cleves, the Mare of Flanders. There is a garden at the back where dogs are welcome.

❸ The Sun Inn
Satnav
RG25 2DJ

Winchester Road, Dummer, Hants.
01256 397 234
www.suninndummer.com
suninndummer@hotmail.co.uk

Orders for food: Monday to Saturday: Noon to 3.00pm and 6.00pm to 9.00pm. Sundays: Noon to 3.00pm.

£

Once a coaching inn on the old A30, it is a cheerful, busy place, where children and dogs are welcome.

❷ The Fox Inn
Satnav
RG25 2BE

Popham Lane, North Waltham, Hants.
01256 397 288
www.thefox.org
info@thefox.org

Orders for food: Weekdays: Noon to 2.30pm and 6.30pm to 9.30pm. Sundays: Noon to 3.00pm and 6.30pm to 8.30pm.

££

An old vernacular Hampshire flint-stone house overlooking quiet farming countryside. It is privately owned and has built up a reputation for home-sourced food, and has made special provision for children. A heated patio for inclement weather and log fires when in extremis.

For the Chestnut Horse, take the A34 towards Sutton
Scotney and then the A33 towards Basingstoke. At the
end of the dual carriageway bear right on the A3047
towards New Alresford. After two miles turn right to
Easton. For The Bush Inn take the A31 towards Alresford
and left where signed Ovington.

Places of interest
The Grange (18thC) EH – 8 miles

Ⓐ Chestnut Horse

Satnav
SO21 1EG

Easton, Winchester, Hants.
01962 779 257
www.thechestnuthorse.com
info@thechestnuthorse.com

Orders for food: Daily: Noon to 2.30pm and 6.00pm to
9.30pm. Sundays: Noon to 8.00pm.

££

A tenanted pub of Hall &
Woodhouse, so a good
range of beers. An old
16th-century building
with low beams, log fires
and a cheerful
atmosphere. Traditional
cooking and friendly
service. Outside seating
on a terrace at the rear
for summer days.

ⓑ Tichborne Arms

Satnav
SO24 0NA

Main Road, Tichborne, Hants
01962 733 760
www.tickbornearms.co.uk
tichbornearms@xln.co.uk

Orders for food: Weekdays: Noon to 2.00pm and
6.00pm to 9.00pm. Saturday: Noon to 2.30pm and
6.00pm to 9.00pm. Sunday: Noon to 2.30pm.

                                                    ££

A thatched Free House country pub in this tiny historic
village. Patrick Roper forsook the life of a successful
City solicitor for a more tranquil rural existence but you
can dine there surrounded by pictures and prints of
great historic judges of former times. The Real Ales are
changed regularly and served direct from the barrel. The
food is seasonal and cooked to order but sandwiches on
brown, white or ciabatta bread are available for those in
a tearing hurry which would be a pity. You will have to
ask Patrick about the history of the Tickborne Dole.

JUNCTIONS 8/9 TO 49

The M4, which is 121 miles long, is the fourth longest motorway in the UK. It is a direct link from London to South Wales and interconnects with the M5 north of Bristol. The first part, the Chiswick Flyover, was opened in 1959 and the last part was completed in 1973 terminating in a rather bleak part of South Wales. In between it passes through some of the most varied scenery in southern England.

It is divided into three sections.

WINDSOR TO HUNGERFORD

JUNCTIONS 8/9 TO 14

This section of the motorway follows the Thames to Reading and from there the River Kennet to Newbury. From there it rises to the open expanses of the Marlborough Downs.

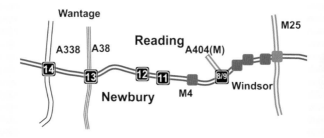

M4

8/9 High Wycombe, Henley A404(M)
Maidenhead A308(M)

Take the spur road A308(M) to the roundabout and then
the A330 for Ascot and Bracknell. Left again at the village
green and the Belgian Arms is 200 yards on the left.

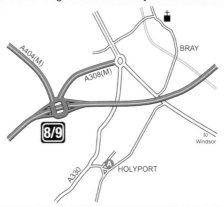

Places of interest
Dorney Court HHA – 5 miles

Ⓐ The Belgian Arms

Satnav
SL6 2JR

Holyport Street, Holyport, Berks.
01628 634 468
www.thebelgian.co.uk
thebelgianarms@live.co.uk

Orders for food: Daily: Noon to 2.30pm and 6.30pm to
9.30pm. Sundays: Noon to 3.00pm.

££

A popular pub on the edge of the village green by a duck

pond. There is a large garden
where you can sit and dogs
can play (on leads). Fish
specials daily. It has been
enlarged to provide a dining
area. You will have to ask why
it is called The Belgian Arms.

At the roundabout turn left to Three Mile Cross, but avoid getting onto the dual carriageway. This junction has been recently upgraded and is therefore more complicated.

Places of interest
Silchester (Calleva Atrebartum) – 7 miles
Stratfield Saye HHA – 5 miles

The Swan

Satnav **RG7 1AT**

Basingstoke Road, Three Mile Cross, Berks.
01189 883 674
www.theswan-3mx.co.uk

Orders for food: Weekdays: Noon to 2.30pm and 7.00pm to 9.30pm. Saturdays: Noon to 2.00pm and 7.00pm to 9.30pm. Sundays: Noon to 3.00pm.

££

Traditional privately owned Free House for the past 30 years with dining areas and bar meals, all washed down with a large selection of real ales. There is outside seating in a prize winning ornamental garden, and a restaurant with a covered patio, with its own bar.
The resident Irish Wolfhound, Mr Niall, is the mascot of London Irish RFC.

At the first roundabout turn right to Theale, which is a surprisingly attractive little town. It is so named as it was the second night's stop out of London for wagoners and was called The Ale. It certainly seems to have more than its fair share of pubs and hotels, so if the one mentioned below is full, there are alternatives.

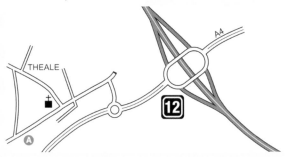

Places of interest
Engelfield House Garden HHA – 3 miles
Basildon Park (1776-1783) NT – 7 miles

Ⓐ The Volunteer

Satnav
RG7 5BX

65 Church Street, Theale, Berks.
01189 302 489
www.thevolunteertheale.co.uk
volunteertheale@btinternet.com

Orders for food: Weekdays: Noon to 2.30pm and 6.00pm to 9.00pm. Saturdays: Noon to 9.00pm
Sundays: Noon to 4.00pm.

 £

A traditional pub which serves fresh home cooked meals There is outside seating with part of it under a verandah. An interesting collection of military and sporting prints.

For Chieveley bear first left off the A34 going towards Oxford. The Olde Red Lion is on the left as you come into the village. The Red House is further away. From the A34 going south, take the old A4 to Hungerford. Turn left at the end of the park estate wall of Benham Vallence.

Places of interest
Highclere Castle HHA – 6 miles

A Ye Olde Red Lion

Green Lane, Chieveley, Berks.
01635 248 379
www.yeolderedlion.com
redlion@toucansurf.com

Satnav
RG20 8XB

Orders for food: Weekdays: Noon to 2.30pm. 6.30pm to 9.30pm. Sundays: Noon to 3.00pm. 6.30pm to 9.00pm.

££

An old country pub with dining areas around a central bar. A friendly atmosphere enhanced by prints and pictures. A constant feature in the guide owing to its value for money.

B **The Red House**

Main Road, Marsh Benham, Berks
01635 582 017
www.theredhousepub.com

Satnav
RG20 8LY

Orders for food: Daily: Noon to 9.30pm.

£££

A privately owned elegant restaurant cum pub in a thatched house with a dining room overlooking a garden near the River Kennet. A la carte menu using local produce, as well as a Chef's fixed price menu. Afternoon teas are served as a special treat.

Follow the B4000 towards Lambourn. The Pheasant Inn
is a few hundred yards on the right. The Tally Ho is
south of the junction.

Places of interest
Ashdown House (c1690) NT – 9 miles

Ⓐ The Pheasant Inn

Satnav
RG17 7AA

Ermin Street, Shefford Woodlands, Berks.
01488 648 284
www.thepheasant-inn.co.uk
enquiries@thepheasant-inn.co.uk
Orders for food: Daily: Noon to 2.30pm and 7.00pm to
9.00pm.

££

It has always been a popular rendezvous and now has
eleven modern, comfortable and quiet bedrooms. There

is a restaurant with an
excellent chef and a
convivial bar where
members of the racing
fraternity meet. It is a
pleasant and congenial
place.

Ⓑ The Tally Ho

Satnav
RG17 0PP

Newtown, Hungerford, Berkshire
01488 682 312
www.thetallyhohungerford.co.uk
welcome@thetallyhohungerford.co.uk
Orders for food: Monday to Thursday: Noon - 2.00pm
and 7.00pm - 9.00pm. Friday & Saturday: Noon -
2.00pm and 6.30pm - 9.30pm. Sunday: Noon to
3.00pm.

££

A traditional country pub, now owned by the village
community. It serves freshly cooked, homemade food
with locally sourced ales by a cosy log fire! The Tally Ho
provides a warm welcome all year round and is ideally
located for the motorway traveller, being only 800 yards
from junction 14.

Our Pub

"There has been a pub on
the site where The Tally
Ho stands today from the
1750s.

More recently, the pub's
future was threatened
when it was bought by
property developers who
planned to turn the

building into three homes. Members of the village formed a
working party and campaigned to save the pub - the last meeting
place in the village. A website was created and 350 people
signed the online petition. Many were not locals, but regular
visitors who used the pub as a stopping off point during journeys
along the M4.

A limited company was formed and after negotiations with the
developer, the Tally Ho was purchased. Currently there are over
a hundred shareholders from locations all over the world. The
pub was then completely re-designed with a new kitchen, new
loos and even a new bar, built by one of the villagers. Many
hundreds of volunteer hours were put into achieving this."

HUNGERFORD TO
SEVERN BRIDGE

JUNCTIONS 15 TO 22

From Junction 15 to Junction 18, the motorway passes through the southern part of the Cotswolds. From there, it descends down onto the flood plain of the River Severn.

Swindon is now a modern commercial town. Chippenham, once a picturesque market town, has now been modernised out of all recognition. Bath, south of Junction 18, is world famous for its Georgian architecture.

In 1996 the second Severn Bridge was completed to cope with the increased traffic. The old bridge crossing was then renamed the M48 and the new section became the M4. The M49 link to Avonmouth is best avoided if seeking a meal.

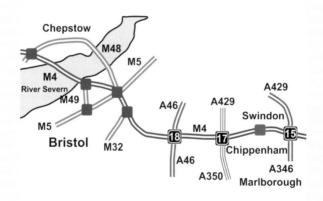

From the junction take the A346 to Marlborough. At the top of the hill the Chiseldon House Hotel will be to the right on the outskirts of the village. The Parklands Hotel, which is brown-signed on the road, is in Ogbourne St George. You might be invigorated by the famous Lay Line from Cornwall to Suffolk which passes through the church.

Ⓐ Chiseldon House Hotel

Satnav **SN4 0NE**

New Road, Chiseldon, Wilts.
01793 741 010
www.chiseldonhouse.com
welcome@chiseldonhouse.com

Orders for food: Daily: Noon to 2.00pm and 7.00pm to 9.00pm. Sundays: Noon to 2.00pm and light evening meals.

£££

A late Georgian manor house with a friendly and relaxed atmosphere set in three acres of gardens. Comfortable restaurant, bar and lounge.

❸ Parklands Hotel

Satnav **SN8 1SL**

Ogbourne St George, Nr Marlborough. Wilts
01672 841 555
www.parklandshoteluk.co.uk
mark@parklandshoteluk.co.uk

Orders for food: Daily: 9.00am to 9.00pm.
Breakfasts from 7.00am on weekdays.

££

A family run friendly village hotel with a separate dining
room where full breakfasts to light meals are served. In
the bar lounge there is a range of real ales on tap whilst
the bedrooms form part of the building. The village is
overlooked by the Marlborough Downs.

The Hit or Miss in Kington Langley could be missed,
which would be a pity but take the single track road 100
yards south of the Junction marked Dales Lane. The
Jolly Huntsman is brown signed. The New Inn is harder
to find, but follow the signs. The same could be said for
Grittleton, before regaining the motorway at Junction 18.

Places of interest
Bowood House (c1720-1760) HHA – 6 miles
Lacock Abbey (1232-1540) NT – 7 miles
Corsham Court (1582) HHA – 9 miles

Ⓐ The Hit or Miss

Satnav
SN15 5NS

Days Lane, Kington Langley, Wilts.
01249 758 830
natsgough@aol.com

Orders for food: Weekdays: Noon to 2.30pm and
6.30pm to 9.30pm. Sundays: Noon to 7.30pm.

 ££

A popular village pub and restaurant dating from the
18thC and thus with
low beams in this
scattered hamlet.
There is a friendly
welcome to all,
including dogs and it
has an imaginative
menu. A good
ambiance as it is
privately owned.

❶ New Inn

Satnav
SN15 5HA

Hen Lane, Upper Seagry, Wiltshire
01249 721 083
www.thenewinnseagry.co.uk
thenewinnseagry@hotmail.co.uk

Orders for food: Weekdays: Noon to 2.00pm and
6.00pm to 9.00pm. Sundays: Noon to 2.00pm. Closed
on Mondays.

                      £

A locals' pub in the village, with beams, red carpets and

wooden tables. The
outside seating is
enclosed with lattice
fencing as the houses
are close by. Pleasant,
helpful and cheerful
atmosphere. Yes to
children. Dogs on leads.

❸ Neeld Arms

Satnav
SN14 6AP

The Street, Grittleton, Wilts.
01249 782 470
www.neeldarms.co.uk
info@neeldarms.co.uk

Orders for food: Monday to Saturday: Noon to 2.00pm
and 6.30pm to 9.30pm. Sunday Noon to 2.30pm and
7.00pm to 9.00pm.

£££

A Free House owned by
Charlie & Boo West. It is
still a locals' village pub,
but now has a restaurant
with traditional meals. A
cheerful and friendly
place and ideal for those
coming to Mary Howard's
Gift Fair at Hullavington.

M4 **17** Chippenham A350
Cirencester A429

D The Jolly Huntsman

Satnav
SN14 6JB

High Street, Kington St Michael, Wilts
01249 750 305
www.jollyhuntsman.com
thejollyhuntsman@aol.com
Orders for food:
Daily: 11.30am to 2.00pm and 6.30pm to 9.30pm.
Sundays: Noon to 2.00pm and 7.00pm to 9.00pm.

 £

A popular locals' pub in this attractive village. It is well known for its Real Ales of which there are six different varieties as well as a range of ciders. An extensive menu is available and meals can be taken in the bar or restaurant areas. Well behaved children and dogs are welcome.

E Stanton Manor Hotel

Satnav
SN14 6DQ

Main Street. Stanton St. Quintin. Wilts.
01666 837 552
www.stantonmanor.co.uk
reception@stantonmanor.co.uk
Orders for food: Daily: Noon to 2.00pm and 6.00pm to
9.30pm. Sundays: Noon to 2.00pm and 7.00pm to 9.00pm.
Breakfasts available on request.

 ££

A privately owned hotel, set in 7 acres of garden. With 23 bedrooms, most in a modern annexe. Children and dogs by arrangement. Bar meals are served but there is the Burghley Restaurant, so named as the house was once owned by Queen Elizabeth's Chief Minister.

The Bull seems further than it is. The Tollgate is down
the road from The Crown if tea or a light lunch beckons.

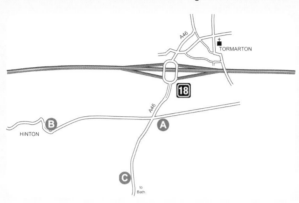

Places of interest
Dyrham Park (1691) NT – 1 mile
Horton Court (c1690) NT – 7 miles

Ⓐ The Crown

Satnav
SN14 8HZ

Dyrham, Glos.
01225 891166
www.thecrowntolldown.uk
thecrowntolldown@wadworths.co.uk

Orders for food: Mondays to Saturdays: Noon to
3.00pm and 6.00pm to 9.00pm. Sundays: Noon to
8.00pm. Breakfast: Weekdays: 7.30am to 9.30am.
Weekends: 8.00am to 10.00am.

 ££

A country pub-cum-restaurant
just two minutes from
Junction 18. Once a
coaching stop in the 1700s, it
still gives a friendly welcome
and serves home-cooked
meals . Outside seating
where dogs are allowed.

B **Bull Inn**

Satnav
SN14 8HG

Main Road, Hinton, Glos.
01179 372 332
www.thebullathinton.co.uk
reservations@thebullathinton.co.uk
Orders for food: Tuesday to Friday: Noon to 2.00pm
and 6.00pm to 9.00pm. Saturdays: Noon to 9.30pm.
Sundays: Noon to 8.30pm. Mondays: 6.00pm to 9.00pm.

    ££

A friendly village pub
with two large fireplaces
for winter nights, a
restaurant and a large
garden. All food is
cooked on the
premises. It is highly
rated by other motorists.

C **Tollgate Teashop**

Satnav
SN14 8LF

Oldfield Gatehouse, Dyrham, Glos.
01225 891 585
www.tollgateteashop.com
Orders for food: Daily: 9.30am to 5.00pm. Summer
weekends: 9.30am to 6.00pm. Closed on Mondays.

   £

A small privately owned teashop for the past 23 years,
which was once a Toll House. Good breakfasts, light

lunches and old
fashioned teas with
clotted cream. Outside
seating in the garden
at the rear with views
over to the Welsh hills
and the bridges over
the Severn.

MAGOR TO PONTARDDULAIS

JUNCTIONS 23 TO 49

As the map suggests there are few places where it is worth leaving the motorway to eat. There are however, plenty of places of interest to see to make up for it.

Caerleon off Junction 24 is the site of Isca, the Roman base of the II (Augusta) Legion raised in Spain. Nearby is Caerwent, the old Roman capital of the Silures. The castle in Cardiff is built on the walls of the Roman fort, whilst to the north there is the medieval Castell Coch. Both were restored by the 3rd Marquess of Bute in the 19th century with the help of the architect William Burges.

Some six miles beyond Castell Coch to the east are the imposing ruins of Caerphilly Castle, mute evidence of the occupation of Wales by Edward I.

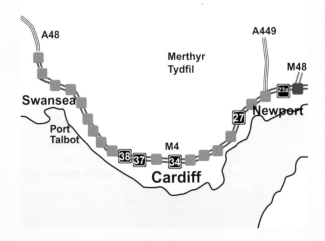

M4  **23a** Magor B4245 Caldicot

Either bear right at the traffic lightsaandn then left or straight on down, return and turn right. To get back to the motorway you will have to go left and go round the roundabout to return.

 Wheatsheaf
The Square, Magor, S.Wales.
01633 880 608
wheatsheafinn@msn.com

Satnav
NP26 3HN

Orders for food: Monday to Saturday: Noon to 9.30pm.
Sundays: Noon to 3.00pm.

££

A leasehold from Enterprise Inns. It is some two hundred

years old with large modernised open-plan dining areas and a restaurant beyond. Home cooked meals and friendly service.

Take the B4591 road north to Risca and Abertillery.
After about 1 mile The Rising Sun will be on your left
behind a red telephone box.

Places of interest
The 14 canal locks

The Rising Sun

Satnav
NP10 9AQ

1 Cefn Road, Rogerstone, S.Wales
01633 895 126
www.therisingsunnewport.co.uk
russel@therisingsunnewport.co.uk

Orders for food: Daily: Noon to 2.15pm and 5.30pm to
9.00pm. Sundays: Noon to 7.00pm.

££

A family-run pub with a
good reputation. It has
a two-storey
conservatory at the
rear of the restaurant,
with two large bars
elsewhere. The menu
is imaginative with self-
service at lunch. A
surprise to find a
deservedly popular
place which looks unassuming at first sight.

M4

37 Porthcawl A48, Pyle, Port Tabot

At Junction 37 take the short dual carriageway south. At the roundabout turn left. After the next roundabout, turn right on to a very narrow road to Kenfig where the pub is on your right. From the west come off at Junction 38 and take the A4283.

Places of interest

Margam Abbey(1147). Margam Orangery (1790), the longest in the UK.

Ⓐ Prince of Wales

Satnav
CF33 4PR

Ton Kenfig, Nr Porthcawl, Mid Glam.
01656 740 356
www.princekenfig.com
prince_of_wales@btconnect.com

Orders for food: Weekdays: Noon to 2.30pm and 6.00pm to 8.30pm. Sundays: Noon to 2.15pm. Mondays: No meals.

£

A plain-looking building but with a fascinating past. It is a 16th-century family-owned pub which has been

a mortuary for shipwrecked bodies. It was also the old Parliament and Court House for the now lost port of Kenfig which was swept away by a tsunami in 1550. It is reputed to be the most haunted pub in Wales but it is, however, a very friendly place with a warm welcome.

JUNCTIONS **1** TO **31**

The M5 is 168 miles in length and was built in stages, the first part being completed in 1969 and the last in 1976. It was designed to link the Midlands with the South West via Bristol. It is one of the few motorways which has no connection with London. Considering that it passes through some of the prettiest of the English countryside, the needs of motorists are poorly served.

It is divided into three sections.

DROITWICH TO TEWKESBURY
JUNCTIONS **1** TO **10**

A boring stretch of motorway until you get to the south of Worcester.

The roundabouts tend to confuse, but look out for the signs to Droitwich

Places of interest
Hanbury Hall NT – 4 miles

Ⓐ Robin Hood

Satnav
WR9 0BS

Rashwood Bank, Rashwood, Worcs.
01527 869 302
www.vintageinn.co.uk/therobinhooddroitwich
Orders for food: Daily: Noon to10.00pm.
Sundays: Noon to 9.30pm.

££

A Mitchell & Butler-owned pub with tiled and wooden flooring and a well-laid-out dining area. It is deservedly well known to the passing motorist. Outside seating and a beer garden at the rear, where dogs are allowed. It has recently changed management.

From the junction take the A 4538. Left at the
roundabout and after a mile, at a sharp left-hand bend,
turn right at a badly-signed junction to Crowle Green.

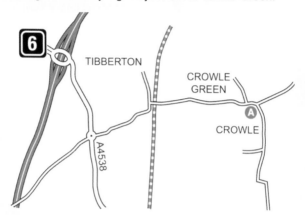

Ⓐ **Old Chequers**

Crowle Green, Crowle, Worcs.
01905 381 275
www.oldchequersinn.co.uk
oldchequersinn@btinternet.com

Satnav
WR7 4AA

Orders for food: Tuesday to Saturday: Noon to 2.30pm
and 6.00pm to 9.00pm.
Sundays: Noon to 2.30pm.

££

A 400 year-old village free house pub which David and
Lesley Newbrook have
taken over. Spacious
dining room and a large
bar area. Friendly
service with an
imaginative menu and
real ales. A large garden
for warm days where
you can also play
boules.

You can practically see The Swan from the junction. At the first roundabout take a right and The Swan is behind the high hedge and trees to the right. For Kempsey take the A38 towards Tewkesbury. The Talbot is opposite the Walter de Cantalupe.

Places of interest Worcester Cathedral.

Ⓐ The Swan

Satnav
WR5 2RL

Main Road, Whittington, Worcs
01905 351361
www.swanatwhittington.com
info@swanatwhittington.com

Orders for food: Monday to Friday: 9.00am to 9.30pm
Saturday and Sunday: 10.00am to 9.30pm. Breakfast:
Weekdays: From 9.00am. Weekends: From 10.00am

££

The Swan is part of a group of three other places in the neighbourhood. Airy open plan seating surrounds a central bar. There is a beer garden at the rear and a children's playground. Deservedly popular, as it is within a few hundred yards of the junction. The staff are friendly and efficient, who will provide a newspaper to read if asked.

Ⓑ The Walter de Cantelupe Inn

Satnav
WR5 3NA

Main Road, Kempsey, Worcs.
01905 820 572
www.walterdecantelupe.co.uk
info@walterdecantelupe.co.uk

Orders for food: Tuesday to Thursday: 6.00pm to a 9.30pm. Fridays and Saturdays: Noon to 2.30pm. Sundays: Noon to 7.30pm. Closed Mondays, except Bank Holidays.

££

Named after a 13th-century Bishop of Worcester, this old merchant's house, under the aegis of the proprietor who was trained in France, offers everything to the weary traveller, including supper after the official closing hour. Local produce including wine,beer and fruit.

ⒸThe Talbot

Satnav
WR5 3JA

Main Road, Kempsey, Worcs.
01905 828 473
Orders for food: Daily: Noon to 9.00pm.
Sundays: Noon to 5.00pm

£

A tenanted locals' pub in the village. It is well known for its real ales and different varieties of cider. There is ample seating in the dining areas around a bar where homemade English food is available. Well behaved dogs are welcome as indeed are children.

Tewkesbury Abbey is one of the finest early Norman churches in the country so this is an excuse to go and see it. Take the road to the town and the Theoc House will be on your right when you come into the centre before you get to a mini roundabout with a Market Cross.

Places of interest
Tewkesbury Abbey (1089)

Ⓐ **Theoc House**

Barton Street, Tewkesbury, Glos.
01684 296562
www.theochouse.co.uk
info@theochouse.co.uk

Satnav
GL20 5PY

Orders for food: Daily: 8.30am to 10pm. Breakfast from 8.30am.

££

An independently owned bar/ restaurant which has become popular with those viewing the Abbey because of its friendly, efficient service with a wide-ranging menu. There is limited seating outside on the pavement and well-behaved children and dogs are welcome.

TEWKESBURY TO WELLS

JUNCTIONS **11** TO **21**

This stretch takes you from Gloucester, with its historic cathedral where Edward II is buried, to the south of Bristol.

The motorway passes through pleasant countryside and there are interesting houses and places to visit along the River Severn. Just north of the bridge over the River Avon Kings Weston House, designed by Sir John Vanbrugh, can be seen on the hills to the east. You can divert along the Avon Gorge into Bristol with its restored dockside and where the SS Great Britain is dry-docked after being brought back from the Falklands in 1970.

During the summer the stretch south from the M4 intersection to the bridge over the Avon can get gridlocked.

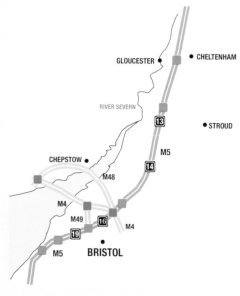

For the Bell take the A38 towards Bristol. After 1 mile
turn right to Frampton on Severn. The inn is on the edge
of the village green. The Frombridge Mill is straight on at
the roundabout down a private road.

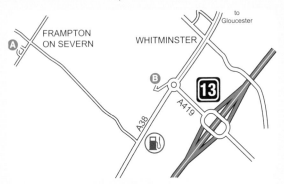

Places of interest
Frampton Court Pte – 3 miles
Wildfowl Centre (Slimbridge) – 5 miles

Ⓐ The Bell Inn

Satnav
GL2 7EP

The Green, Frampton on Severn, Glos.
01452 740 346
www.thebellatframpton.co.uk
relax@thebellatframpton.co.uk

Orders for food: Daily: Noon to 9.00pm.

££

An old coaching inn from the 1700's but now updated with

cheerful and friendly staff.
Bar snacks are served
together with lunches,
dinners, morning coffee
and afternoon tea in the
dining areas. There is
plenty of outside seating
and children may look at
some rare breed farm
animals.

ℬ Frombridge Mill

Satnav
GL2 7PD

Frombridge Lane, Whitminster, Glos.
01452 741 796
www.frombridge-mill-whitminster.co.uk
6452@greeneking.co.uk

Orders for food: Sundays to Thursdays: Noon to
9.00pm. Fridays and Saturdays: Noon to 10.00pm

££

As the name implies this was a working water mill and
indeed the River Frome flows past on either side. The
interior is now stripped of machinery so it makes an
ideal place to have lunch or dinner, sit outside if the
weather permits or even go for a walk. Dogs and well
behaved children welcome.

Come off the motorway and drive on the A38. For the Anchor Inn, bear right on the B4061 to Thornbury. The Gables Hotel is a short distance on the left. Turn right at a crossroads as you come into the town signed Oldbury-on-Severn. In the village turn left to Kington. The Anchor is on the left as you go over a stream. This area is steeped in history and atmosphere and is well worth the additional time. The Gables Hotel is a short distance from the roundabout.

Places of interest
Berkeley Castle (12th C) HHA - 5 miles

Ⓐ The Anchor Inn

Satnav
BS35 1QA

Church Road, Oldbury-on-Severn, Glos.
01454 413 331
www.anchorinnoldbury.co.uk
info@anchorinnoldbury.co.uk

Orders for food: Weekdays: 11.30 am to 2.00pm and 6.00pm to 9.00pm. Saturdays: 11.30am to 2.30pm and 6.00pm to 9.00pm. Sundays: Noon to 3.00pm and 6.00pm to 9.00pm.

 £

A locals' pub in this old village by the River Severn. It has

a traditional public bar and a comfortable lounge. A dining area at the rear of the house overlooking the garden. Awarded Best Value Pub of the Year.

Ⓑ The Gables Hotel

Satnav
GL12 8DL

Bristol Road, Falfield, Glos
01454 260 502
www.thegablesbristol.co.uk
mail@thegablesbristol.co.uk

Orders for food: Daily: Noon to 10.00pm.
Breakfasts: Weekdays: 7.00am to 9.30am.
Saturdays and Sundays: 8.00am to 10.00am

 ££

The Gables, part of the Best Western hotels group, is
a modern building but with pitched roofs and black and
white timber framing. It is just half a mile from the
junction so handy for those who want a coffee or
else a quick lunch either in the bar or in the restaurant.
An added plus is that you can have breakfast there.
Although alongside the A38 it is soundproofed so a
quiet night's sleep can be had.

Take the A38 dual carriageway to Thornbury. Turn left to
Almondsbury, opposite the Swan Inn on the right. Bear
left down the hill, turn right at a Memorial Cross. Turn right
again after the church. Coming from the north, turn right
down an unmarked road just before the 30mph sign. .

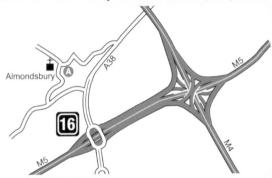

Ⓐ The Bowl Inn

Satnav
BS32 4DT

Church Road, Lower Almondsbury, S.Glos.
01454 612 757
www.thebowlinn.co.uk
bowlinn@sabrain.com

Orders for food: Monday to Friday: Noon to 2.30pm
and 6.00pm to 9.30pm. Saturday: Noon to 9.30pm.
Sundays: Noon to 7.30pm

£££

A village inn with a
restaurant and recently
refurbished bedrooms
under the beamed roof.
The original cottages were
built in 1146 to house the
builders of the church and
it is now a friendly,
efficient hostelry with a
good menu and service.

Bar meals are available and can be eaten while
admiring the view over the Severn to Wales.

Take the A369 and turn right onto the road to Portbury. For the Black Horse, follow signs to Clapton in Gordano. Both roads are narrow. In the village, turn sharp left up a lane and the pub is on the right.

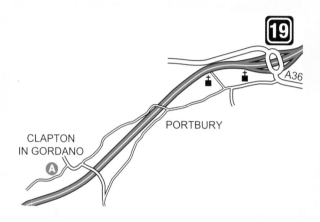

ⓐ The Black Horse

Satnav
BS20 7RH

Clevedon Lane, Clapton in Gordano, Som.
01275 842 105
www.thekicker.co.uk
theblackhorse@talktalkbusiness.net

Orders for food: Monday to Saturday: Noon to 2.00pm. Sundays: No meals served.

£

A charming old-fashioned pub serving bar meals such

as bowls of homemade soup, as well as a full-blown meal. A large garden at the rear where children are welcome. Inside low beams and snugs with flagstone floors. A cheerful and bustling atmosphere and frequented by the locals.

WELLS TO EXETER

JUNCTIONS 21 TO 31

The motorway winds over the Mendip Hills before crossing the flat levels of Sedgemoor and the subject of the recent floods.

Glastonbury, famous for the supposed site of the Holy Grail and also for the annual music festival, is within reach of the motorway.

Taunton is an attractive county town, with a good antique market.

The motorway ends south of Exeter and continues as a dual carriageway to Plymouth and Cornwall.

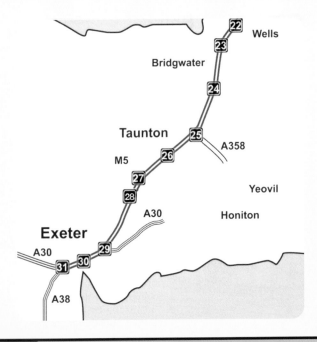

It is relatively simple. From the north take the A38, and the White Cottage is on the left at the end of the village of West Huntspill. Get back onto the M5 at junction 23. Going north, come off at junction 23 on to the A38 and afterwards rejoin the motorway at junction 22.

HIGHBRIDGE

A38

HUNTSPILL

R Huntspill

WEST HUNTSPILL

Ⓐ The White Cottage

Satnav
TA9 3RQ

Old Pawlett Road, West Huntspill, Som.
01278 794 692
colinfrost@aol.com

Orders for food: Wednesday to Saturdays: Noon to 1.45pm and 6.30pm to 8.45pm. Sundays: Noon to 1.30pm and 6.30pm to 8.30pm. Closed Mondays and Tuesdays.

£

A privately owned restaurant as opposed to a pub so no noisy background, but low-beamed with old-fashioned charm and a helpful and friendly staff. They were very busy when I passed by but the soup was good and homemade. A garden but no outside meals.

The Puriton Inn is signed just off the junction on the left.

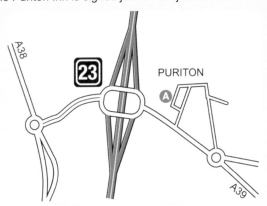

Places of interest
Glastonbury Abbey – 13 miles

 Puriton Inn

Puriton Hill, Puriton, Som.
01278 683 464
www.thepuritoninn.co.uk
info@thepuritoninn.co.uk

Satnav
TA7 8AF

Orders for food: Daily: 11.30am to 9.00pm. Sunday:
Noon to 9.00pm.

££

A 200 year old village
pub just off the
motorway. It has a
dining area with two
bars serving real
ales. Outside, there
is a children's
playground with
outdoor seating
where dogs are
allowed and a shelter
for smoking.

This is one of the easiest places to find. From the motorway, go left at the roundabout on the A38 and the Compass Inn is just 100 yards south on the left. There is a Filling Station on the roundabout.

The Compass Tavern

Satnav
TA6 6PR

Taunton Road, North Petherton, Som.
01278 662 283
www.thecompassinn.co.uk
martgill@btconnect.com

Orders for food: Daily: Noon to 2.45pm and 6.00pm to 9.00pm.
Sundays: Noon to 9.00pm.

££

A converted mock-Tudor building, with large open beamed dining areas, but pay heed to the notices to "Mind your step or mind your head". Friendly atmosphere with home cooked meals and real ales.

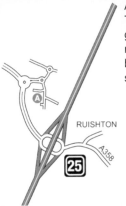

RUISHTON

At the junction head towards
Taunton. At the first roundabout
go right and again right at the
next. The Hankridge Arms will
be on the right surrounded by
supermarkets.

Places of interest
Hestercombe Gardens (1750s
and Gertrude Jekyll)
HHH – 5 miles

The Hankridge Arms

Satnav
TA1 2LR

Hankridge Way, Taunton, Som.
01823 444 405
www.thehankridgearms.com
bookings@thehankridgearms.com

Orders for food: Monday to Saturday: Noon to 2.00pm
and 6.00pm to 9.00pm. Sundays: Noon to 2.30pm and
6.00pm to 8.30pm.

£££

Now a restaurant with a bar area, it was once an
Elizabethan farmhouse of some importance, rescued
from dereliction at some considerable cost. No sooner
was it completed
than it was
surrounded by a
shopping precinct.
It is, however, a
comfortable and
friendly place,
which offers a two-
course lunch at £10
(except on
Sundays).

Both the alternative roads to reach the Merry Harriers are single track for the first mile so take the shorter route via Blackmoor. When you reach the top of the Blackdown Hills, turn left signed Blagdon Hill. The inn is about two miles on the right.

Places of interest
Cothay Manor Gardens (1480) HHA – 4 miles

 The Merry Harriers

Forches Corner, Clayhidon, Devon
01823 421 270
www.merryharriers.co.uk
merryharriers.bookings@btinternet.com

Satnav
EX15 3TR

Orders for food: Tuesday to Saturday: Noon to 2.00pm and 6.30pm to 9.00pm. Sundays: Noon to 3.00pm.

££

An old coaching inn which stands where highwaymen once held sway. The greeting is much friendlier now

with low beams and inglenook fires adding to its character. Fresh fish from Brixham is on the menu and an array of local beers on tap. In summer there is a large shaded garden, with a play area for children. It has been awarded Best Licensee of the Year and in the Top Ten UK Pubs.

Ⓑ **Old Well Garden Centre** Satnav **EX15 3ES**

Waterloo Cross, Uffculme, Devon.
01884 840 873
www.theoldwell.co.uk
theoldwellgardencentre@hotmail.co.uk

Orders for food: Monday to Saturday: 9.00am to 4.30pm.
Sundays and Bank Holidays: 10.00am to 4.00pm.
Mini Breakfasts available.

It is a family owned Garden Centre which has grown
and enlarged over the years. It now has a coffee shop
where the coffee is excellent, the service friendly and
the opportunity to buy cakes, scones and pies, all of
which are home baked on the premises. In addition
there is a gifts and crafts shop.

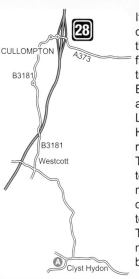

If coming from the north get off at the junction and drive through Collompton. At the first roundabout after the town turn left on the B3181 signed Exeter. Over the M5 and after Westcott turn left signed Langford, Plymtree and Clyst Hydon. At a T junction turn right and follow the sign to The Five Bells. To continue to Exeter you can try navigating the Devon lanes or use Satnav but advisable to return the way you came. This applies for those driving north. More than five minutes but worth the extra time.

Ⓐ **The Five Bells Inn**

Satnav
EX15 2NT

Clyst Hydon, Devon.
OI884 277 288
www.fivebells.uk.com
info@fivebells.co.uk

Orders for food: Daily: Noon to 2.00pm and 6.00pm to 9.00pm. Sundays: Noon to 9.00pm.

££

Newly acquired as a sister pub to the Jack in the Green, the Five Bells is a charming Grade II listed, 16th century, thatched Devon inn. There are four dining areas including the bar serving pub favourites and bar

meals. There is a family games room for rainy days and a spacious beer garden when the sun shines.

M5 | **29** | Exeter
Honiton A30

Take the A30 towards Honiton. After 300 yards, turn left onto B3174 and pass Clyst Honiton and Exeter Airport. Keep on this road for about three miles to Jack-in-the-Green and the pub will be on the left. They are building a new town alongside the B3174 so it could be slower.

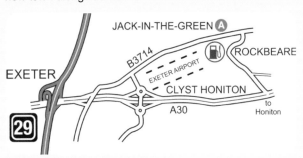

Ⓐ Jack in the Green Inn

Satnav
EX5 2EE

Main Road, Rockbeare, Devon
01404 822 240
www.jackinthegreen.uk.com
info@jackinthegreen.uk.com

Orders for food: Daily: 11.30am to 2.00pm and 6.00pm to 9.00pm. Sundays: Noon to 9.00pm.

  ££

A free house which has been there for several centuries. It has been modernised with a lounge bar and a

restaurant in the old part. Leather sofas in the sitting areas and outside seating in an enlarged courtyard for summer days. It has been voted in the Top 50 Gastropubs for the last three years.

For the Blue Ball – up to the first roundabout and return.
Turn left before the motorway. For the Digger's Rest take
the B3052 for half a mile and turn right to Woodbury
Salterton. Darts Farm is in Topsham over the river.

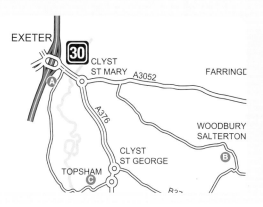

Ⓐ Blue Ball Inn

Clyst Road, Sandygate, Devon
01392 873 401
www.blueballpub.com
info@blueballpub.com

Satnav
EX2 7JL

Orders for food: Monday to Thursday: Noon to 2.30pm
and 6.00pm to 9.00pm. Friday and Saturday: Noon to
2.30pm and 6.00pm to 9.30pm. Sunday: Noon to 8.00pm.

                                          ££

An attractive 18th-century
pub-cum-restaurant which
has had a makeover.
Scrubbed tables, tiled floors,
low-beamed ceilings and
home cooking give a homely
feeling. A carpeted,
comfortable dining room has
been added. Coffee and teas
available. There is a large
garden, but dogs are not welcomed.

ⓑ Digger's Rest

Main Road, Woodbury Salterton, Devon
01395 232 375
www.diggersrest.co.uk
bar@diggersrest.co.uk

Satnav
EX5 1PQ

Orders for food: Daily: Noon to 2.00pm and 6.00pm to 9.00pm.

££

A fifty-year-old cider house, now a pub-cum-restaurant

in the centre of the village with a thatched roof, low beams and a cheerful fire. The name derives from an Australian who owned it some forty years ago. What remains is the good cooking, efficient service and, depending on who is serving, a reminder of its Australian antecedents.

ⓒ Darts Farm

Darts Farm Village, Topsham, Devon
01392 878 205
www.dartsfarm.co.uk
info@dartsfarm.co.uk

Satnav
EX5 2JU

Orders for food: Daily: 8.00am to 4.00pm.

£

Darts Farm is well known as a place with everything any motorist might wish to buy to enhance the holiday in the West Country. For immediate needs the restaurant will

produce meals from breakfast time to High Teas until 6.00pm. There is also a "Fish Shed" for Fish and Chips until 8.00pm from Tuesday to Saturday. Dogs welcome outside.

The Nobody Inn is 4 miles from the A38 and the Exeter Race Course road. After three miles turn left opposite the Haldon Belvedere. The last part is through narrow Devon lanes so beware of oncoming buses. Switch on your Sat Nav to avoid getting lost.

This could be the lollipop of the M5 at the end of a long journey.

Ⓐ Nobody Inn
Main Road, Doddiscombsleigh, Devon
01647 252 394
www.nobodyinn.co.uk
info@nobodyinn.co.uk

Satnav
EX6 7PS

Orders for food: Weekdays: Noon to 2.00pm and 6.30pm to 9.00pm. Fridays and Saturdays: Noon to 2.00pm and 6.30pm to 9.30 pm. Sundays: Noon to 3.00pm and 7.00pm to 9.00pm.

£££

A free house tucked away in deep countryside. It has a large bar for lunches and a restaurant for evening meals and a friendly service. The wine list states that there is a range of over 200 wines and some 250 whiskies.

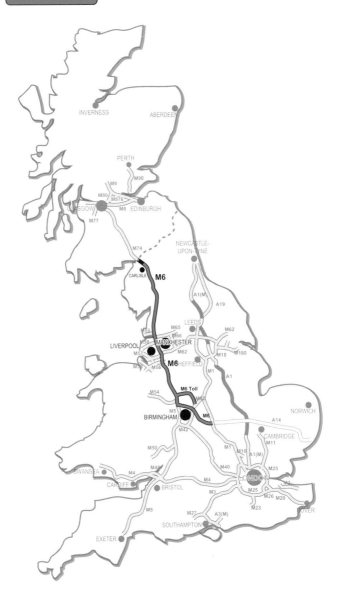

RUGBY TO CARLISLE

JUNCTIONS 1 TO 44

The M6 is one of the longest motorways, being some 180 miles in length. The first trial section of a motorway was built as the Preston Bypass in 1958 and then became part of the M6. It was built over a period of years, starting in 1962 and the last stage was finished in 1972. The section passing through the Lake District is particularly picturesque. The link over the Scottish Border has now been completed to motorway standard.

It is divided into three sections.

RUGBY TO STAFFORD

JUNCTIONS 1 TO 14

This section of the motorway is dull and when combined with the inevitable snarl-up at Spaghetti Junction it becomes downright tedious. It gets better just south of Stafford. The opening of the new M6(Toll) has improved matters, but hurry on as best you can.

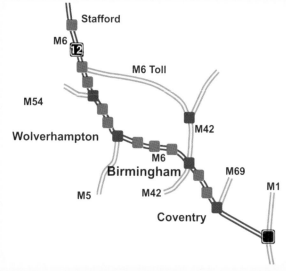

Weston Park is more than 5 minutes from the Junction
but it is a straight road as the A5 is the old Roman
Watling Street. Penkridge is to the right at the first
roundabout on the A449 and the Littleton Arms is on the
left as you come into the centre of the town. If driving
from the north you can come off at Junction 13 which is
signed Stafford (S&C) A449.

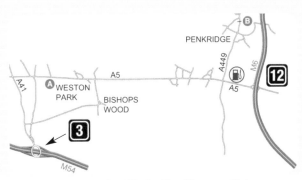

A Granary Grill & Deli

Satnav
TF11 8LE

Weston Park, Nr Shifnal, Shropshire
01952 852 107
www.weston-park.com
enquiries@weston-park.com

Orders for food: Monday and Tuesday: Noon to
2.30pm. Wednesday to Saturday: Noon to 2.30pm and
6.30pm to 9.30pm. Sundays: Noon to 3.30pm.

£££

Something a bit different! It was formed from the granary
of Weston Park, a magnificent 17th Century ancestral
home that is well worth seeing. The welcome in the

Granary (built in 1767) is friendly
and efficient. You can see the
adjoining art gallery if you have
time or have a coffee in the Deli
& Cafe. The walled garden is
open where you can take a
wander round the orchards and
meet the chickens.

ⓑ The Littleton Arms

Satnav
ST19 5AL

St Michaels Square, Penkridge, Staffs
01785 716 300
www.thelittletonarms.co.uk
littletonarms@gmail.com

Orders for food: Mondays to Fridays: Noon to 2.30pm and 5.00pm to 9.30pm (Fridays 10.00pm). Saturdays: Noon to 10.00pm. Sundays: Noon to 8.00pm.

 ££

It started life as the village ale house but was rebuilt in Georgian times as a Coaching Inn. It has since then been updated and is now a cheerful and efficient hostelry. The décor however remains Georgian in that it is not fussy and overdone. It is by the main road so you can watch the world go by if it is warm enough to sit outside. Well behaved children welcome and dogs, but not in the dining areas.

STAFFORD TO PRESTON

JUNCTIONS 15 TO 32

Stoke-on-Trent is (or was) the home of pottery, most of which is attractive, but the same could not be said for the town itself. Nearby Barlaston Hall was built in 1756 by the architect Sir Robert Taylor for the Wedgwood family as their home and factory. It was shamefully neglected by the firm, until saved at the last moment by SAVE Britain's Heritage in 1978.

The countryside in Cheshire is pleasant enough, but once over the Manchester Ship Canal the innate good manners in the north of England become more apparent.

Barthomley is one mile from the junction. Do not take the A500 to Crewe! Follow the signs B5078 to Alsager. After 1 mile turn left to Barthomley. The White Lion is on the left of a junction opposite the church. If you want an evening meal they will direct you to The Hand and Trumpet in Wrinehill which is 2.5 miles away.

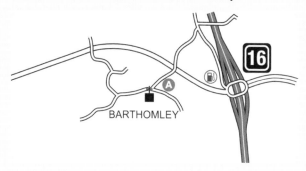

Ⓐ White Lion Inn

Audley Road, Barthomley, Ches.
01270 882 242
www.whitelionbarthomley.com
laurawhitelion@hotmail.co.uk

Satnav
CW2 5PG

Orders for food: Monday to Saturday: Noon to 2.00pm. Sundays: Noon to 2.30pm. No evening meals.

££

A Grade II listed building which is really an old-fashioned locals' tavern with a bar in one room and an inglenook fire in the other. It was built in 1614 and has not changed much since then. An interesting experience and old-world hospitality.

Take the A534 Congleton road. After about a mile there are traffic lights at a crossroads with the A50. The Zest is on the other side of the crossroads on the left. If that is full, the Bears Head in Brereton is an alternative.

Places of interest
Little Moreton Hall (1504-1610) NT – 6 miles

🅐 Zest Restaurant

Newcastle Road, Arclid, Ches.
01477 500 440
www.visitzest.co.uk
zest.arclid@gmail.com

Satnav
CW11 2SN

Orders for food: Weekdays: Noon to 2.30pm and 5.00pm to 11.00pm. Saturdays: Noon to midnight. Sundays: Noon to 11.00pm with a 50 item buffet.

                                                        ££

And now for something to spice up a long car journey. The Zest specialises in a range of Indian food. Clean, spacious and with efficient service, it makes a change from the normal.

B Old Hall

High Street, Sandbach, Cheshire
01270 758 170
www.oldhall-sandbach.co.uk
old.hall@brunningandprice.co.uk

Satnav
CW11 1AL

Orders for food: Weekdays: Noon to 10.00pm.
Sunday: Noon to 9.30pm

££/£££

The Old Hall is hardly a pub being a Grade I listed
building built in 1656 for the Lords of the Manor. It is
however a friendly, efficient and comfortable place to
have a meal, a cup of coffee and provision is made for
those in a hurry. Well behaved children and for that
matter dogs are welcome. A large garden for fresh air.

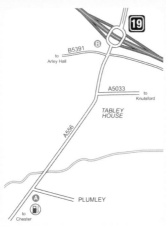

The Smoker at Plumley may seem to be a bit far for those in a hurry, but worth it.
The Windmill is just off the junction and will provide you with a quick meal.

Places of interest
Arley Hall & Gardens (19thC) HHA – 5 miles
Tatton Park (18th & 19thC) NT – 3 miles
Tabley House (18thC) University of Manchester – 2 miles

The Smoker

Satnav
WA16 0TY

Chester Road, Plumley, Ches.
01565 722 338
www.thesmokerinn.com
info@thesmokerinn.com

Orders for food: Monday: 6.00pm to 7.30pm. Tuesday to Friday: 10.00am to 9.15pm. Saturday: 10am to 2.15pm and 6.00pm to 9.15pm. Sundays: 10am to 7.30pm. Breakfasts available from 10.00am.

 ££

A well-known hostelry which has been modernised into a comfortable restaurant and a bar area with an imaginative menu. For those in a hurry there is a sandwich menu. In addition there is a large garden, open fires and plenty of seating. You will have to ask why it is called The Smoker.

❷ The Windmill Inn

Satnav
WA16 0HW

Chester Road, Tabley, Knutsford,
Cheshire
01565 625 885
windmill@thewindmillattabley.co.uk

Orders for food: Monday to Saturday: 8.00am to
10.30am. Noon to 9.00pm. Sunday: 8.00am to 10.30am.
and 12.30pm to 5.00pm.
Breakfast: From 8.00am.

   ££

The Windmill has reappeared in the guide as it has been
refurbished and the service is efficient. Open-plan
seating, facing a long bar. I borrowed a paper to read
and the soup was good. A handy stopover, especially for
breakfast.

From Junction 27 take the B5250 towards Eccleston.
The Corner House is at the apex of a fork in the road at
the end of Wrightington Bar. On the way there the White
Lion is on the right if you are in a hurry.

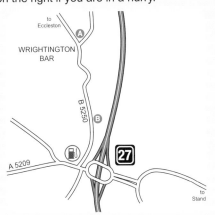

Ⓐ The Corner House

Satnav
WN6 9SE

9 Wood Lane, Wrightington Bar, Lancs.
01257 451 400
www.cornerhousewrightington.co.uk
info@cornerhousewrightington.co.uk

Orders for food: Daily: Noon to 2.30pm and 5.00pm to
9.00pm. Saturday and Sunday: Noon to 9.30pm

                                          £££

It was previously called the Mulberry Tree and has
changed hands. There
is a large open dining
area by the bar but
there is a separate
restaurant. Traditional
British cooking but with
a twist. Efficient service
and a pleasant change
from the motorway.
Best to book over a
weekend.

ⓑ The White Lion

Satnav
WN6 9RE

117 Mossy Lea Road, Wrightington, Lancs.
01257 425977
www.thewhitelionlancs.co.uk
info@thewhitelionlancs.co.uk

Orders for food: Daily: Noon to 9.00pm
Saturday and Sunday: 10.00am to 9.00pm.
Breakfast: From 10.00am.

£

A Marstons owned pub with a friendly welcome from
Matt and Ellie Furzeman. It is the centre of activity,
especially after 5.00pm when the locals are returning
from work. It is justly renowned for having eight real ales
on offer in keeping with its tradition as an Ale House.
A beer garden at the rear for warm summer evenings.

Come off at the motorway interchange on to the M55. From Junction 1 drive into Broughton. At the traffic lights turn right to Longridge on the B5269. The Italian Orchard is brown-signed on the right just before you go under the motorway.

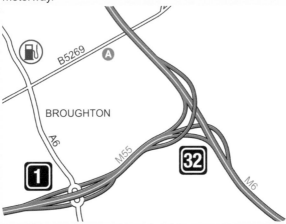

Italian Orchard

Satnav
PR3 5DB

96 Whittingham Lane, Broughton, Lancs.
01772 861 240
www.italianorchard.com
info@italianorchard.com

Orders for food: Monday to Saturday: Noon to 2.00pm and 6.00pm to 10.30pm. Sundays: Noon to 10.00pm.

££

A modern open-plan restaurant, partly under a double-height timber roof and a cosy bar area. Linen tablecloths and napkins, but it is reasonably priced and a two course lunch without wine could be £12 per head. Extensive grounds with a long drive.

M6

PRESTON TO CARLISLE

JUNCTIONS **33** TO **45**

This section is the most scenic of any of the motorways in the UK as it climbs up past Kendal with views of the Lake District to the west and the Pennines to the east and the Pennines to the east. Once over Shap, the highest point of the motorway, it passes Penrith which is a picturesque market town and then down to Carlisle. From there the M6 links with the M74 into Scotland.

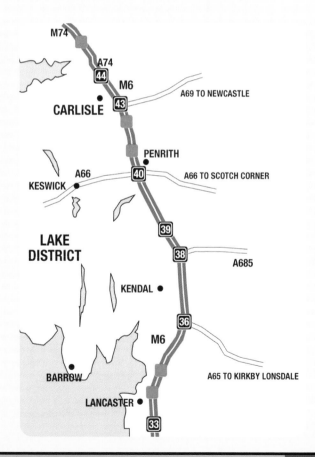

GALGA TE

A6

to
Garstand

The Canalside Craft Centre is on the left when you come into Galgate.

For the Bay Horse turn left at the roundabout on the A6 towards Garstang. After 400 yards bear left, where it is brown-signed to the Bay Horse, for a mile. If coming from the south on the A6 bear right at Potters Brook as signed.

Ⓐ **Canalside Craft Centre**

Satnav
LA2 0LQ

Main Road, Galgate, Lancs.
01524 752 223
info@canalsidecraftcentre.com

Orders for food: Daily: 11.00am to 3.00pm (winter) or 4.00pm (summer).

                                              £

A craft centre with a coffee shop serving everything from toast to a full meal.
An ideal spot for those just wanting a light lunch and an airing for dogs or children along the canal bank. Homemade meals, soups and cakes a speciality.

Ⓑ The Bay Horse Inn

Satnav
LA2 0HR

Bay Horse Lane, Forton, Lancs.
01524 791 204
www.bayhorseinn.com

Orders for food: Tuesday to Saturday: Noon to 2.00pm
and 6.30pm to 9.00pm. Sundays: Noon to 3.00pm. and
6.00pm to 8.00pm. Closed on Mondays.

££

It is a secluded 18th-century pub-cum-restaurant down
a quiet country lane. It has a well-deserved reputation
for food and a friendly ambiance with a cheerful bar, log
fires and a separate dining room.

M6

36 S.Lakes, Kendal, Barrow A590
Kirkby Lonsdale, Skipton A65

From the junction take the A590 towards Kendal. After three miles bear left to Barrow still on the A590. Almost immediately take a small road to the right marked Sizergh. The Strickland Arms is ahead of you after 400 yards, near the gates into Sizergh Castle (NT) the seat of the Strickland family. The Low Sizergh Barn just a few hundred yards away is a farm shop, tea room and craft gallery if you want to find a present. There is also the NT shop at Sizergh Castle.

Places of interest
Levens Hall (16thC) and Gardens (1614) HHA- 1 mile
Sizergh Castle (14th & 16thC) NT-1mile

Ⓐ Strickland Arms

Satnav
LA7 7NW

Main Road, Sizergh, Cumbria
01539 567 432
thestricklandarms@yahoo.com

Orders for food: Monday to Friday: Noon to 2.00pm and 6.00pm to 9.00pm.
Saturday and Sunday: Noon to 8.30pm.

££/£££

An excellent stopover, now run by Martin Ainscough. Large airy rooms in keeping with the age of the house and a friendly welcome. Plenty of outside seating in the garden. We were half an hour late in arriving but they managed to produce a good lunch nevertheless.

ⓑ Low Sizergh Barn

Sizergh, Kendal, Cumbria
01539 560 426
info@lowsizerghbarn.co.uk

Satnav
LA8 8DZ

Orders for food: Noon to 5.00pm for lunches and high teas. Breakfast 9.30am to 11.30am

  ££

Sizergh is old Norse for summer pasture and cows have been looked after here since the 13th century. Although cows are still much in evidence the old barns have now been converted into a craft centre selling a range of clothes and gifts as well as a café/restaurant where you can have breakfast, lunches and cream teas. It is certainly a change from the normal stop-over.

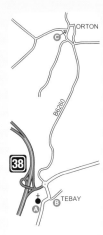

M6 — 38 Kendal, Brough A685 / Appleby B6250

Dual carriageways lead off the motorway on to a roundabout. Take the A685 towards Kendal for The Cross Keys and the Old Barn Tearoom. For Kennedys Chocolates take the B6260 to Orton which is an attractive 17th Century village. Kennedys will be on the left of the road in the village.

Places of interest

The Roman fort and road at Low Borrowbridge. (If you can get to them!)

Ⓐ The Cross Keys Inn

Satnav
CA10 3UY

Tebay, Penrith, Cumbria
01539 624 240
www.crosskeystebay.co.uk
reservations@crosskeystebay.co.uk

Orders for food: Monday to Friday: Noon to 3.00pm. and 5.00pm to 9.00pm. Saturday and Sunday: Noon to 9.00pm Times may vary with the seasons.

££

It is a friendly and well run place. There is a restaurant

but bar meals are available. A large garden behind for warm days where you can sit and admire the hills of the Lake District on the other side of the valley.

Ⓖ Kennedys Fine Chocolates

The Old School, Orton, Cumbria   Satnav
01539 624781   **CA10 3RU**
www.kennedys-chocolates.co.uk
kennedys.chocolates@btinternet.com
Orders for food: Monday to Saturday 9.00am to 4.30pm
Sundays: 11.00am to 4.30pm

 £

Another old School house, but this one is now Kennedys
Chocolate Factory. The chocolates are all hand-made
on the premises, with over 80 different varieties of
fillings, and make an ideal present should you be on
your way to stay with friends. It also has a café for light
refreshments, as well as teas.

An easy junction.
Picnics on a fine day.

Places of interest
Shap Abbey EH –
3 miles

A The Greyhound Hotel

Satnav
CA10 3PW

Main Street, Shap, Cumbria
01931 716 474
www.greyhoundshap.co.uk
enquiries@greyhoundshap.co.uk

Orders for food: Daily: Noon to 9.00pm. Sundays:
Noon to 8.00pm. Breakast is available.

£

Apparently Bonnie
Prince Charlie
spent a night here
on his way south in
1745. It has
recently changed
hands, but we
received a friendly
welcome. For those
spending the night,
beware of the main
railway just behind.

For the Gate Inn take the road to Eamont Bridge and turn right on the Tirril road for one mile. For the Kings Arms take the A66 towards Keswick. Left at the first roundabout by the Rheged Centre on the A592 and first right to Stainton. Left at the crossroads in the village.

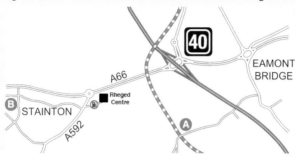

Places of interest
Dalemain (15thC and 19thC) – 3 miles
The Toffee Shop, Penrith – 1 mile

Ⓐ The Gate Inn

Satnav
CA10 2LF

Old Road, Yanwath, Cumbria
01768 862 386
www.yanwathgate.com
enquiries@yanwathgate.com

Orders for food: Daily: Noon to 2.30pm and 6.00pm to 9.00pm.

££

A privately owned pub-cum-restaurant dating from 1683, which was originally a toll gate, in a quiet secluded lane with whitewashed exposed stone walls. It has a dining room and bar, as well as outside seating. It has been awarded the Cumbrian Dining Pub of the Year for the past six years. A good stopover.

Ⓑ Kings Arms

Satnav
CA11 0EP

The Green, Stainton, Cumbria
01768 862 778

www.kingsarmspub.com
kingsarmspub.stainton@live.co.uk

Orders for food: Mondays to Fridays: Noon to 2.00pm and 6.00pm to 9.00pm. Saturdays and Sundays: Noon to 9.00pm.

£

A family run rural pub built in 1721. It provides a range of homely fare with a whiff of vinegar on the chips. A friendly welcome and you get what you see. Outside seating in a covered area on hot days.

After one mile on the A69 turn right to Wetheral and there follow the signs to the railway station.

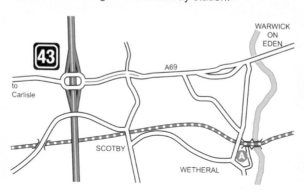

Places of interest

Carlisle Castle and Cathedral – 3 miles

Ⓐ Crown Hotel

Station Road, Wetheral, Cumbria
01228 561 888
www.crownhotelwetheral.co.uk
info@crownhotelwetheral.co.uk

Satnav
CA4 8ES

Orders for food: Daily: 10.00am to 9.00pm.
Breakfast available.

££/£££

The Crown Hotel dates back to the old coaching days and is now a modern and efficient country hotel. Waltons Bar is an ideal place for a quick meal with a friendly welcome and local real ales such as Corby are on tap. A large garden for fresh air and an indoor swimming pool.

From the Junction take the A689 towards Brampton.
Bear left at the first roundabout. After about 2 miles turn
right where signed Low Crosby. The Stag Inn will be on
the left in the village.

 Hadrian's Turf Wall.

Stag Inn

Satnav
CA6 6QN

Main Street, Low Crosby, Cumbria
01228 573 210
www.staginncrosby.com
joannaharper@aol.com

Orders for food: Monday to Friday: Noon to 2.00pm and
7.00pm to 9.00pm. Saturday and Sunday: Noon to 9.00pm

£

A tenanted pub of Jennings, it has been an Ale House
for the past two hundred years. The low ceilings and
small rooms give
a feeling of
timelessness.
The locally grown
food is cooked in a
traditional manner.

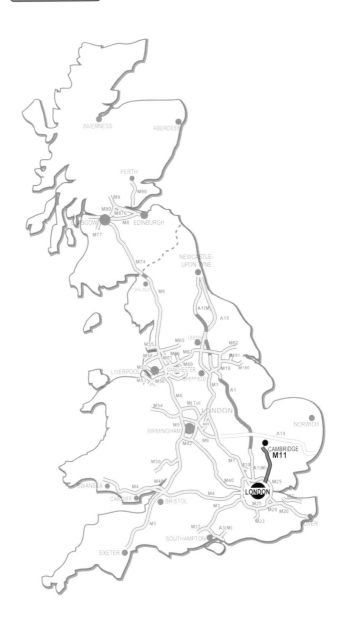

JUNCTIONS 7 TO 14

For those travelling north from the Channel Tunnel it is a good alternative to the M1 as it links the M25 with the A1(M) at Huntingdon.

The southern section goes past the town of Harlow and Stansted Airport. Further north the countryside is pleasant enough and passes some attractive towns such as Saffron Walden. At Duxford is the Imperial War Museum and the American Air Museum.

Cambridge of course is a must for anyone who has never been there.

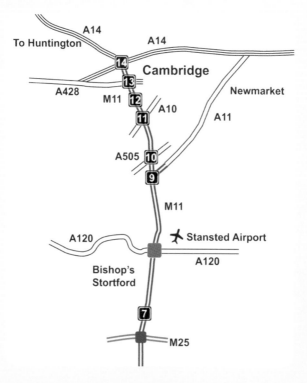

The roundabout is controlled by lights. Take the Chelmsford road and almost immediately turn off to the left on a small road which is marked St. Clare Hospice and Hastingwood.

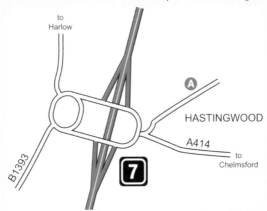

Ⓐ The Rainbow and Dove   Satnav   CM17 9JX

Hastingwood Road, Hastingwood, Essex
01279 415 419
www.rainbowanddove.com
rainbowanddove@hotmail.co.uk

Orders for food: Daily: Noon to 2.30pm and 6.30pm to 9.00pm. Sundays: Noon to 4.00pm.

      £

Now a free house which is a rural pub-cum-restaurant. It is said to date from the 15th century and was certainly

an Ale House in 1645 when Cromwell's soldiers stopped there. There is a large garden with a barn for functions. Inside a warm fire during the winter.

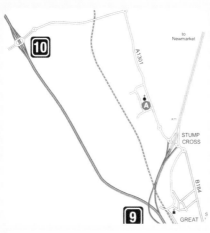

Going north come off at junction 9 and bear left on to A1301 to Cambridge. Left to Hinxton and head for the church. Rejoin the motorway at junction 10. Coming south, it is vice versa.

Places of interest
Audley End House (Jacobean) EH – 5 miles

Ⓐ The Red Lion

High Street, Hinxton, Cambs.
01799 530 601
www.redlionhinxton.co.uk
info@redlionhinxton.co.uk

Satnav
CB10 1QY

Orders for food: Monday to Thursday: Noon to 2.00pm and 6.30pm to 9.00pm. Fridays and Saturdays: Noon to 2.30pm and 6.30pm to 9.30pm. Sundays: Noon to 3.00pm and 7.00pm to 9.00pm. Breakfast: Weekdays: 7.30am to 8.30am. Weekends: 8.30am to 9.30am.

££

A 16th-century pub in this attractive village, with eight bedrooms set apart. A well-deserved reputation for home cooking in the restaurant and bar. Friendly atmosphere and a warm welcome. You can take a walk along the river bank by the old watermill.

Take the A505 towards Royston. A mile after the Imperial
War Museum, turn right to Thriplow, which is an attractive
village. Left at the T-Junction by the village shop.

Places of interest

The Imperial War Museum and American Air Museum.
1 mile

Ⓐ **The Green Man**

Lower Street, Thriplow, Herts.
01763 208 855
www.greenmanthriplow.co.uk
manager@greenmanthriplow.co.uk

Satnav
SG8 7RJ

Orders for food: Tuesday to Saturday: Noon to 2.00pm
and 7.00pm to 9.00pm. Sundays: Noon to 2.00pm.
Mondays: Closed.

                                    £

Literally a locals' pub as it has
just been bought out by the
village. The exterior has been
painted white, to make a
change from green. The interior
has wooden tables and chairs
in both rooms. A selection of
Real Ales and plenty of outdoor
seating.

From the junction take the A10 towards Royston. After about half a mile turn left onto the B1368 to Newton, which is about one and a half miles away. The Queen's Head is to the left on the edge of the village green.

Ⓐ Queen's Head

Satnav
CB22 7PG

Fowlmere Road, Newton, Cambs.
01223 870 436
Orders for food: Daily: Noon to 2.15pm and 7.00pm to 9.30pm. Christmas and Boxing Days - Closed.

££

A pleasant and friendly hostelry which has been in the same family ownership for 50 years. Good food in the

original dining room which has a blackened ceiling. A locals' bar will give you a warm welcome. An interesting collection of watercolurs.

Burwash Manor Tearooms

New Road, Barton, Cambridge
01223 364 821
www.burwashmanor.com
thebarntearooms@googlemail.com

Satnav
CB23 7EY

Orders for food: Mondays to Fridays: 10.00am to
4.30pm. Saturdays: 10.00am to 5.00pm. Sundays:
11.00am to 5.00pm. Breakfasts: From 10.00am.

££

A family owned business which has developed from being
just a working farm into a range of country pursuit shops in
the converted barns covering a spectrum of activities. The
Barn Tearooms offer welcome refreshment and for those
in more of a hurry the Food Hall will provide you with a
takeaway meal. Plenty of space for children to play.

The picturesque village of Grant-chester was made famous by the First World War poet Rupert Brooke's poem Grantchester which had the line, "Is there honey still for tea?"

Places of interest
Wimpole Hall (18thC Style) NT – 6 miles

Ⓐ The Red Lion

Main Street, Grantchester, Cambs.
01223 840 121
www.theredlion-grantshester.co.uk
4129@greeneking.co.uk

Satnav
CB3 9NQ

Orders for food: Daily: 10.00am to 10.00pm.
Sundays: 10.00am to 9.00pm.

££

A welcome surprise to find this recently renovated and large inn in this world famous village. It is friendly and efficient with large airy dining areas and a bar overlooking a large garden. A gopod setting to sit and comtemplate.

Coming from the south, come off at junction 13 and
rejoin at junction 14. For those coming from the north,
get off at junction 14, but it will require a degree of map
reading. However it is well worth the effort to get to
Madingley.

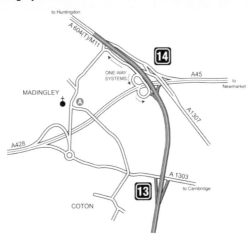

Ⓐ The Three Horseshoes

Satnav
CB3 8AB

High Street, Madingley, Cambs.
01954 210 221
www.threehorseshoesmadingley.co.uk
3hs@btconnect.com

Orders for food: Mondays -Saturdays: Noon to 2.00pm
and 6.30pm to 9.00pm.. Sundays: Noon to 2.30pm and
6.30pm to 8.30pm.

£££

A privately owned pub-cum-
restaurant, which is efficient
and well run. There is a
restaurant and a long bar with
a conservatory at the rear. It
is surrounded by a pleasant
garden.

M20

M20 London to Folkestone

JUNCTIONS 1 TO 13

The M20, which is 40 miles long, was started in 1961 and finished twenty years later. It is the main motorway from the Channel Ports to link up directly with the M25 and from there the motorway network..

It goes through some very attractive countryside which is still known as the Garden of England.

After Maidstone, with its orchards and oast houses, the M20 climbs the shoulder of the North Weald on its way to London. The M26 spur links up with the southern segment of the M25.

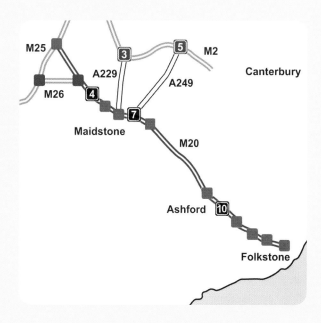

It seems a long way from the junction, but worth the journey.

 The Angel Inn

Main Street, Addington Green, Kent
01732 842 117

Satnav
ME19 5BB

www.theangelinnaddington.co.uk
angeladdington@aol.co.uk

Orders for food: Weedays: Noon to 2.30pm and 6.00pm to 9.30pm. Saturdays and Sunday: Noon to 9.30pm.

££

An atmospheric 14th-century inn with low beams and log fires. Meals are served on hewn wooden tables in areas divided by posts. There is a restaurant in the adjoining converted stables. A large garden, and meals can be taken under a pergola.

Take the A249 to Sittingbourne. After one mile in Detling turn right on the dual carriageway signed Thurnham. It is narrow road so care must be taken. After one mile the Black Horse will be on your right before a cross roads in the village.

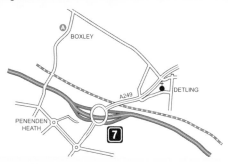

Places of interest
Leeds Castle (12thC) HHA - 4 miles

🅐 The Black Horse Inn

Satnav
ME14 3LD

Pilgrims Way. Thurnham, Kent
01622 737 185
www.wellieboot.net
info@wellieboot.net

Orders for food: Daily: Noon to 9.45pm. Sunday: Noon to 9.30pm. Breakfasts: Daily: 7.00am to 9.30am.

££

An old 18th century building on the Pilgrims Way from Canterbury. It has been converted into a family run hostelry in an area of Outstanding Natural Beauty. The restaurant is comfortable and the bar area is wreathed in hops and in winter there is a log fire and Kentish cask ales are on tap. In summer there is a patio for al fresco dining. For those wanting a longer stay there are 27 chalet style bedrooms in the grounds.

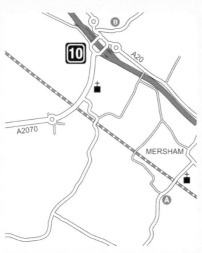

For the Farriers Arms take the A20 towards Folkestone. After a mile, turn right to Mersham. Go through the village and turn right over a bridge and the Farrier's Arms will be on the left. For the Blacksmiths Arms go left for Maidstone and after 100 yards turn right signed Brook. It will be a few hundred yards on the left.

Farrier's Arms

The Forstal, Mersham, Kent
01233 720 444
www.thefarriersarms.com
info@thefarriersarms.com

Satnav
TN25 6NU

Orders for food: Daily: Noon to 3.00pm and 6.00pm to 9.30pm. Sundays: Noon to 8.00pm.

 ££

It has been there from 1606 onwards and has survived happily until recently when it had to be saved by the

villagers clubbing together to buy it. It is therefore truly a locals' pub. It is also a friendly place with low beams, outdoor seating in a large garden at the back and a good atmosphere. A tribute to communal enterprise.

Ⓑ The Blacksmith's Arms

Satnav
TN24 ONA

The Street, Willesborough, Kent.
01233 623 975
www.theblacksmithsarmsashford.co.uk
theblacksmithsarms@outlook.com
Orders for food: Daily: Noon to 2.30pm and 6.00pm to
9.00pm. Sunday: Noon to 4.00pm.

                                                    ££

An old house dating from 1760 and probably the old
smithy, it is now a friendly locals' pub with a beamed
restaurant and a bar where David or Fran will give you
a warm welcome and the real ales are local. It is also
a last port of call for those driving to the Channel Tunnel.
There is a large garden at the rear for summer days.
Our coffee was good.

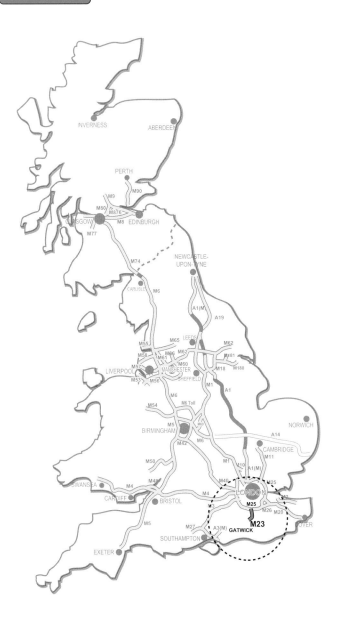

JUNCTIONS 7 TO 11

Built to give quick access from Gatwick Airport to London via Croydon, this 18-mile stretch took nearly four years to complete.

There is no quick way to get to Gatwick by road. The M25 is congested at the best of times and tends to grind to a standstill after 4.30pm in the afternoons.

Gatwick Airport started life as a racecourse in the 19th century before becoming one of the busiest airports in the UK, in spite of only having one runway.

At junction 11 it continues as the A23 to Brighton.

There are several ways to get to the Old House Inn
(which is larger than it would appear on the drawing) on
the B2037. Either follow the plan below or switch on
your Satnav.

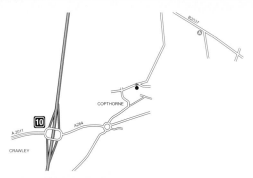

ⒶThe Old House Inn

Effingham Road, Copthorne, W.Sussex
01342 718 529
www.theoldhouseinn.co.uk
info@theoldhouseinn.co.uk

Satnav
RH10 3JB

   £££

Orders for food: Daily: Noon to 3.00pm and 6.00pm to
9.00pm. Sundays: Noon to 4.00pm and 6.00pm to
8.00pm. Breakfasts available from 8.00am if you book in
advance.

A quaint family owned low
beamed house with charm
where Tim and Claudia will
give you a warm welcome.
Small secluded dining
rooms and a bar and
outside there is a large
lawn and garden for
summer days. There are 6
bedrooms so ideal for those
who wisely do not want to trust the traffic jams on the
M25 or else are exhausted by the charter flight home.

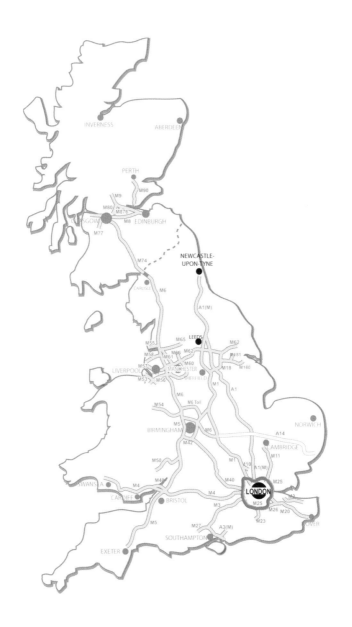

JUNCTIONS 1a TO 30

The idea of an orbital ring road around London was first mooted in 1905. The North Circular Road was built in the 1930s but the South Circular exists and will remain in name only.

In 1975 a decision was made to construct an integrated Orbital Ring Road, which was finally completed in 1986. It was originally intended to have more lanes, but this was deemed to be too expensive. This is now being done at even greater expense but the tailbacks continue.

The M25 does, however, make it easier for visitors from abroad to skirt around London and head north or west.

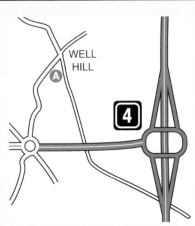

As a junction it is an easy one, but at the roundabout look out for a narrow lane signed Well Hill.

Places of interest

Lullingstone Castle (15thC) HHA – 2 miles
Lullingstone Roman Villa EH – 2 miles

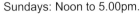

🅐 **Bo Peep Restaurant**

Satnav
BR6 7QL

Hewitts Road, Well Hill, Kent
01959 534 457

www.thebopeep.com
kate@thebopeep.com

Orders for food: Monday to Thursday: Noon to 2.30pm and 6.00pm to 9.00pm. Fridays and Saturdays: Noon to 2.30pm and 6.30pm to 9.30pm.
Sundays: Noon to 5.00pm.

It has been an alehouse since 1549. It is a surprise to find somewhere so close to London and still in the middle of strawberry fields. It has a dining room and a bar for snacks. A well-kept garden and inside a friendly welcome.

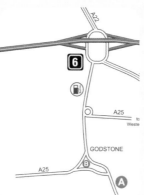

Take the B2236 to Godstone and drive to the end of the village where the Godstone Hotel will be on the left. There is a one way system so going back to the motorway you will pass the the Green Rooms on the right.

Places of interest

Chartwell (Sir Winston Churchill) NT – 8 miles
Squerryes Court (17thC) HHA – 7 miles.
Quebec House (16thC) NT – 8 miles

Ⓐ Godstone Hotel

Satnav
RH9 8DT

High Street, Godstone, Surrey
01883 742 461
www.godstonehotel.com
info@godstonehotel.com

Orders for food: Daily: Noon to 2.00pm and 7.00pm to 10.00pm. Sundays: Noon to 2.30pm.
Breakfasts: 7.30am to 10.00am

A family run hotel in a building which is some 400 years old and with a large garden. Friendly and attentive service and a dining room for a la carte meals.

ⓑ The Green Rooms

Satnav
RH9 8DZ

The Green, Godstone, Surrey
01883 740 407
jeremyappleby@ymail.com

Orders for food: Daily: 9.00am to 5.00pm.
Weekends: 9.30am to 5.00pm.
Breakfasts: From 9.00am.

££

A family run tearoom with a happy atmosphere, especially for children. The food is all home cooked on the spot by Sylvia. Cheerful and a change from the normal.

From the junction, take the road to Woking. Left at the first roundabout and after passing the Ambulance Depot,

turn left at the next roundabout. Almost immediately, turn right to Ottershaw. Through the village, right at a junction on Brox Road and the Castle is 500 yards on your right.

Ⓐ The Castle

Satnav
KT16 0LW

222 Brox Road, Ottershaw, Surrey
01932 872 373
www.the-castle-ottershaw.co.uk
johnandsue@holdfast.net

Orders for food: Monday to Saturday: Noon to 2.00pm and 6.30pm to 9.00pm. Sundays: Noon to 3.30pm.

££

A traditional pub making a welcome change from the

motorway where you will find real ales and homemade food. Of further interest there is a collection of horse brasses and a newspaper dated 4th September 1939 reproting the loss of a torpedoed liner.

A fairly tortuous intersection. Head east to Uxbridge on the M40 for 1.5 miles and come off at Junction 1. Go north on the A40 towards Chalfont St. Giles for 1 mile and bear right on the A412 to Rickmansworth. After 400 yards turn right to Denham. Returning, go under the motorway and rejoin the M40 via two roundabouts and then onto the M25.

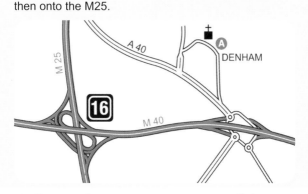

🅐 Swan Inn

Satnav
UB9 5BH

Village Road, Denham, Bucks.
01895 832 085
www.swaninndenham.co.uk
info@swaninndenham.co.uk

Orders for food: Monday to Friday: Noon to 2.30pm and 6.30pm to 9.30pm (10.00pm on Fridays).
Saturdays: Noon to 3.00pm and 6.30pm to 10.00pm.
Sundays: Noon to 9.00pm.

££

The Swan is much frequented both by locals and visitors. I had a friendly welcome and dinner even after 9.30pm on a Sunday evening. The dining room is small and cosy and also serves as a meeting place. A pleasant garden for summer.

After the junction at the first crossroads where there is a filling station go left down Dog Kennel Road. The pub is in the middle of a Common and could be deep in the country.

Places of interest
Chenies Manor House (14th & 15thC) HHA – 3 miles

Ⓐ The Black Horse

Satnav
WD3 5EG

Dog Kennel Rd,Chorleywood Common,Herts.
01923 282 252

Orders for food: Monday to Saturday: Noon to 2.15pm and 6.30pm to 9.00pm. Sundays: Four sittings: Noon, 2.00pm, 4.00pm and 6.00pm.

                                                    ££

A pub since the early 1800s, it now has dining areas

and produces home-cooked specials by log fires in the restaurant or bar areas. There is a children's menu. Dogs have the freedom of the common.

Take the road towards St Albans but at the first roundabout bear left to Chiswell Green and then left to

Potters Crouch. The roads are narrow and not helped by the road widening of the M25 and the resultant lorry traffic. However it is worth the effort.

Places of interest
St Alban's Abbey Church – 3 miles
Verulanium Roman City – 3 miles

Ⓐ The Holly Bush

Satnav
AL2 3NN

Ragged Hall Lane, Potters Crouch, Herts.
01727 851 792
www.thehollybushpub.co.uk
info@thehollybushpub.co.uk

Orders for food: Monday to Tuesday: Noon to 2.00pm. Wednesday to Saturday: Noon to 2.00pm and 6.00pm to 9.00pm. Sundays: Noon to 2.30pm.

££

A 17th-century country pub covered with wisteria near a rural hamlet. It has been run by the same family for 30 years and is filled with old furniture, varnished tables, log fires and a cheerful atmosphere. Outside there is a mature garden where you can grab a moment of relaxation.

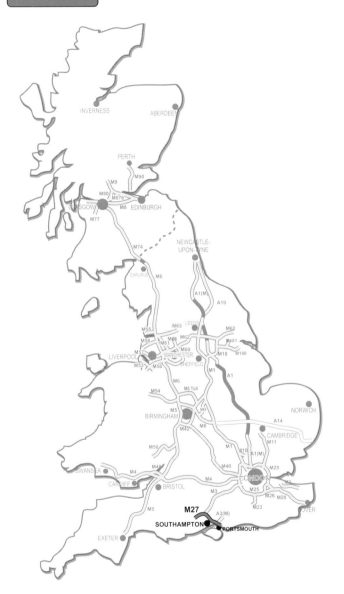

M27

JUNCTIONS 1 TO 12

The M27 which is 27 miles long was built to connect
Portsmouth and Southampton with the M3. It starts as a
motorway at the edge of the New Forest, having been a
dual carriageway from Bournemouth.

The junctions with the M3 and also with the spur M271
to Southampton can be confusing.

At the Portsmouth end it joins up with the A3(M) before
carrying on as a dual carriageway to Chichester,
Brighton and Lewes (with some breaks).

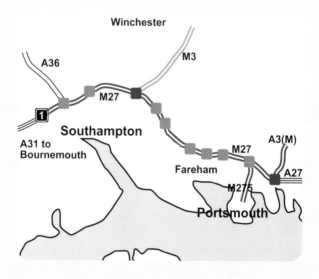

For the White Hart bear left and left again at the first roundabout.
Brook is easy to find at the entrance to the New Forest

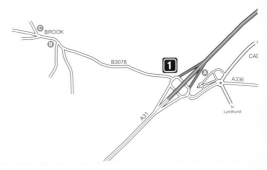

Places of interest:
Rufus Stone – 1 mile
Broadlands House (19C Pte) – 7 miles

The White Hart

Satnav
SO40 2NP

Old Romsey Road, Cadnam, Hants.
02380 812 277
www.whiteharthamp.hcpr.co.uk
white.hartcadnam@homeconnect.hcpr.co.uk

Orders for food: Daily: Noon to 9.00pm

££

It has been a Coaching Inn since the 16th century and still gives a warm welcome to passing motorists with a log fire in the dining room. Outside for summer days there is a secluded garden where dogs are allowed.

B The Green Dragon

Main Road, Brook, Hants.
02380 813 359
greendragon@btconnect.com

Satnav
SO43 7HE

Orders for food: Mondays to Saturdays: Noon to 2.00pm
and 6.00pm to 9.00pm. Sundays: Noon to 6.00pm.

                                          ££

It has been a beerhouse for the
past 200 years and before that
it was used by a coffin maker
and before him by a wheel-
wright. Now it is a cheerful,
friendly place where you can
have a meal in the dining areas
near the bar or else in one of
the smaller rooms.

C The Bell Inn

Main Road, Brook, Hants
02380 812 214
www.bellinnbramshaw.co.uk
bell@bramshaw.co.uk

Satnav
CA11 0EP

Orders for food: Mondays to Saturdays: Noon to 3.00pm
and 6.30pm to 9.30pm Sundays: Noon to
3.00pm.   Breakfast from 7.30am if booked in advance.

   £££

It has been an hotel for the past
200 years and is still family
run. There is a restaurant but
quicker meals can be had in the
bars. A playground and a family
room are available when fathers
(or mothers) are playing golf on
the adjacent course. For the
passing motorist there is
morning coffee or afternoon tea.

JUNCTIONS **1** TO **16**

The first stage to Oxford was finished in 1976, but it took fifteen years to link it to the M42. It was completed in 1991 to take the pressure off the M1 to such an extent that now it is almost as crowded.

From Uxbridge and the junction with the M25 the motorway passes, at present, through the pleasant countryside of the Chilterns.

From there it descends onto the Oxfordshire Plain with the A40 branching off to Oxford and the Cotswolds.

It continues past Bicester and Banbury and then Warwick and Leamington Spa. All of them worth visiting.

Beware of Junction 15 where five roads converge even though it has been improved and modernised.

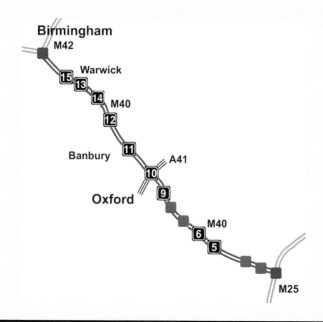

M40 | **5** Stokenchurch A40

Take the A40 towards Milton Common. After 1 mile turn left to Nettlebed. The Fox & Hounds is 4 miles down the road in Christmas Common on the right.

Places of interest
Stonor (12th, 14th & 18thC) HHA – 8 miles
West Wycombe Park (18thC) NT – 7 miles

 # Fox and Hounds

Satnav
OX49 5HL

Main Street, Christmas Common, Oxon
01491 612 599
facebook.com/thetopfox
foxandhoundsxmascommon@email.com

Orders for food: Tuesdays to Fridays: Noon to 2.30pm and 6.00pm to 9.00pm. Saturdays: Noon to 10.00pm. Sunday: Noon to 4.00pm. Closed Mondays.

£££

A brick-and-flint tenanted Brakspear pub, near the Ridgeway in deep Chilterns countryside. The cooking is styled as modern traditional British and the result is good. They also cater for vegans.

Look out for the sign to Lewknor on the right. Do not be put off by all the parked cars on the main road belonging to those who have caught the bus to London. The Shepherds Crook is on the right as you come into Crowell. For the Swan take the A40 towards Milton Common and it is on the right in Tetsworth.

Ⓐ Olde Leathern Bottel

Satnav
OX49 5TW

High Street, Lewknor, Oxon
01844 351 482
www.theleathernbottle.co.uk
juliegordon77@aol.com

Orders for food: Monday to Thursday: Noon to 2.00pm and 7.00pm to 9.30pm. Friday to Saturday: Noon to 2.00pm and 6.00pm to 9.30pm. Sundays: Noon to 2.30pm and 7.00pm to 9.30pm.

££

The Leathern Bottel is 450 years old and is now a pub-cum-restaurant with age-polished floors. It specialises in home cooking and serves coffee and Brakspear Traditional Ales. There is a large garden with seating.

ⓑ Shepherds Crook

Satnav
OX39 4PR

The Green, Crowell, Oxon
01844 355 266
www.the-shepherds-crook.co.uk
jonathan@the-shepherds-crook.co.uk

Orders for food: Weekdays: Noon to 2.30pm and 6.30pm to 9.00pm. Saturdays: Noon to 2.30pm and 6.30pm to 9.30pm. Sundays: Noon to 5.00pm.

 £

A proper village pub with beamed ceilings, brick piers and flagstone floors. Traditional cooking such as kedgeree but fresh oysters are also available. Black Sheep and Timothy Taylor are on tap. The dog biscuits on the bar are for the dogs.

ⓒ The Swan

Satnav
OX9 7AB

Upper High Street, Tetsworth, Oxon
01844 281 182
www.restaurant.theswan.co.uk
restaurant@theswan.co.uk

Orders for food: Mondays to Thursdays: Noon to 3.00pm and 6.00pm to 9.00pm. Fridays: 10.00am to 10.00pm. Saturdays/Sundays: 10.00am to 6.00pm. Breakfasts: From 10.00am.

 ££ or £££

A large Georgian house which has been converted into a restaurant with the outbuildings and gardens as an antique centre. The restaurant is run by Antoine Chretien from Mormandy so the standard is high.

Ⓐ The Plough

Satnav
OX44 7JQ

Main Street, Great Haseley, Oxon
01844 279 283
www.ploughpub.com
ploughpub@hotmail.co.uk

Orders for food: Weekdays: Noon to 2.30pm and
6.00pm to 9.00pm. Saturdays: Noon to 3.00pm and
5.30pm to 9.30pm. Sundays: Noon to 4.00pm.

                                                    £

A thatch-roofed 16th century ale house which has
recently been bought out by the villagers and so, in
every sense of the word, is a village pub again. The bar
is to the left as you come in and a dining room to the
right, which has recently been built, overlooks the
garden. Children and dogs are welcome and the local
dog I met was friendly.

Take the A34 towards Oxford and after about ½ mile
bear left onto the road signposted Weston-on-the-
Green. This will bring you on to the B430 which ends
opposite The Chequers.

 The Chequers

Satnav
OX25 3QH

Northampton Road, Weston-on-the-Green, Oxon
01869 351 743
www.chequerswestononthegreen.co.uk

Orders for food: Monday to Thursday: Noon to 2.30pm
and 6.00pm to 9.00pm. Fridays: Noon to 3.00pm and
6.00pm to 9.30pm. Saturdays: Noon to 9.30pm.
Sundays: Noon to 4.00pm.

££

It has had a makeover,
but still retains a good
atmosphere with low
beams, dried hops and
flagged floors in the
eating areas.

Not such a complicated junction as it looks.

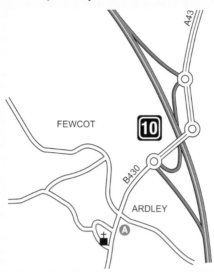

Fox and Hounds

Satnav
OX27 7PE

Main Road, Ardley, Oxon
01869 346 883
foxandhoundsatardley@btinternet.co.uk

Orders for food: Weekdays: Noon to 2.30pm and
5.00pm to 9.00pm. Saturdays: Noon to 9.00pm.
Sundays: Noon to 3.00pm and 5.00pm to 9.00pm.

££

An old coaching inn.
It now has a
restaurant but
serves bar meals as
well. Helpful staff
who produced a
good soup in quick
order when I was in
a hurry.

The Geroge and Dragon is in Chacombe to the left after the second fork. The New Inn is on the left as you come into Middleton Cheney from the A422. The Limes Farm is on the left in Farthinghoe on the Brackley road and the Fox is on th right.

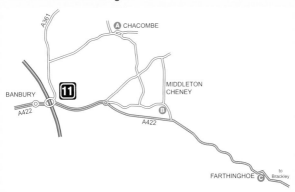

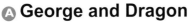

George and Dragon

Silver Street, Chacombe, Northants.
01295 711 500
www.georgeanddragon.org
thegeorgeanddragonchacombe@googlemail.com

Satnav
OX17 2JR

Orders for food: Weekdays and Saturdays: Noon to 2.30pm and 6.30pm to 9.00pm. Sundays: Noon to 4.00pm. Allergies catered for.

££

A low-beamed flagstoned inn, with three dining areas,one with settles and log fires.The bar incorporates the glass. cover of a deep well. The risotto and home made terrine were excellent. Some outside seating on a patio when warm enough.

B The New Inn

Satnav
OX17 2ND

45 Main Road, Middleton Cheney, Oxon
01295 710 399
www.thenewinnpub.co.uk
info@thenewinnpub.co.uk

Orders for food: Mondays to Saturdays: Noon to 2.30pm
and 6.30pm to 9.00pm. Sundays: Noon to 4.00pm.

££

A tenanted 17th century village
pub which John and January
have just taken over so even
better than before. It has a
traditional atmosphere of flagstoned floors, locally sourced
home cooked food and proper
draught beer. There is a
garden at the rear where
children and dogs are welcome.

C Limes Farm

Satnav
NN13 5PB

Main Road, Farthinghoe, Northants.
01295 711 229
www.limesfarm.com
intouch@limesfarm.com

Orders for food: Mondays - Saturdays: 9.00am to
5.00pm. Sundays: 10.00am to 5.00pm.

 ££

The farm has been in the
Deeley family for nearly 200
years and a barn has been
converted into an attractive
double storey café/restaurant
and farm-shop They aim to
keep the old farming
traditions alive and the
welcome is certainly friendly.
You can get breakfast, lunch

or simply stop by for a cake and a cuppa. Be sure to
say hello to the pigs and the very friendly ducks.

Fox at Farthinghoe

Baker Street, Farthingoe, Northants
01295 713 965
www.foxatfarthinghoe.co.uk
enquiries@foxatfarthinghoe.co.uk

Satnav
NN13 5PH

Orders for food: Mondays to Saturdays: Noon to
2.30pm and 6.00pm to 9.30pm. Sundays: Noon to
4.00pm.

££

A refurbished traditional village pub with modern well
furnished bedrooms in the adjacent barn. The flagstone
floored bar serves anything from cappuccinos to real ale
and in three dining areas the parsnip soup and cheese
board can be vouched for as can the friendly service.

The Malt Shovel is brown signed and is near the church in Gaydon. Lighthorne is between Junction 12 and Junction 14 so useful of there is a stoppage on the M40 as the B4100 runs alongside. If you are coming from the north come off at Junction 14 and pass Junction 13 and rejoin at Junction 12. From the south it will be in reverse order. The distance from Junction 14 to Lighthorne is six miles and from Junction 12 it is three miles.

Places of interest

Compton Verney (18thC) CVH Trust – 4 miles
Heritage Motor Museum – 1 mile
Upton House & Gardens (17thC) NT – 9 miles
Edgehill Battlefield – 4 miles

Ⓐ The Malt Shovel Inn

Satnav
CV35 0ET

Church Road, Gaydon, Warks.
01926 641 221
www.maltshovelgaydon.co.uk
malt.shovel@btconnect.com

Orders for food: Daily: Noon to 2.00pm and 6.30pm to 9.00pm.

££

The owners, who used to run hotels in France, are proud to provide real food, which includes handmade meat pies and Real Ales.

Ⓑ Antelope Inn

Satnav
CV35 0BX

Old School Lane, Lighthorne, Warks
01926 651 188
www.antelope-lighthorne.co.uk
info@antelope-lighthorne.co.uk

Orders for food: Monday to Saturday: Noon to 3.00pm
and 6.00pm to 9.00pm. Sunday: Noon to 8 .00pm

                                    ££

The village is deep in the heart of the Warwickshire
countryside and the Antelope has been the village inn
since at least 1849. An old building with flagstones and
individual rooms, one with the bar. A friendly welcome
and attentive service makes this a proper rest from the
motorway traffic.

This is a double Junction. For those coming from the south come off at Junction 13. Turn left and then left again to Bishops Tachbrook. To continue north cross over the motorway at Junction 13 and left at the first round-about to access the motorway at Junction 14. For those coming from the north the same will apply but in reverse order!

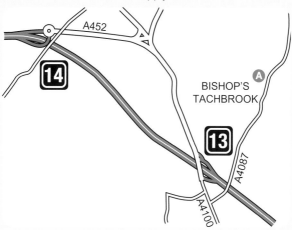

Ⓐ **The Leopard**

Satnav
CV33 9RN

Oakley Wood Road, Bishops Tachbrook, Warks.
01926 426 466
www.leopardinn.co.uk
info@leopardinn.co.uk

Orders for food: Daily: 10.00am to 11.45am and then Noon to 9.00pm. Breakfasts available.

                                         £££

An efficient modernised hostelry which is in the same ownership as the Swan at Whittington. It has a bar where those in a hurry can have a sandwich and a dining room with an imaginative menu for those in a more leisurely mood.

The junction can get congested, but once on the A429 continue south. Barford is now bypassed – so follow the signs to Barford.The Falcon on the A4177 to Solihull is a good stop over for breakfasts.5 miles away

Places of interest
Charlecote Park (1558) NT – 7 miles

The Granville@Barford   Satnav **CV35 8DS**

Wellesbourne Road, Barford, Warks.
01926 624 236
www.granvillebarford.co.uk
info@granvillebarford.co.uk

Orders for food: Weekdays: Noon to 2.30pm and 6.00pm to 9.30pm. Saturdays: Noon to 9.30pm. Sundays: Noon to 5.00pm.

££

A former coaching inn, which has recently changed hands, now a restaurant/bar which was voted Pub of the Year by the readers of Warwickshire and Worcestershire Life. The food is locally sourced and the staff are helpful and friendly. Bar snacks are also available. A large garden with seating underneath canopies.

M42

BROMSGROVE TO TAMWORTH

 **M42**

JUNCTIONS **2** TO **14**

Completed in 1986, it is in effect the southern and eastern part of the Birmingham Ring Road, with the M6 and the M5 completing the circuit. It is a useful link for those using the M40 and also for those who are hoping to avoid the delays at Spaghetti Junction by using the M5.

Beyond Junction 11 it continues as a dual carriageway, with numbered junctions, until it joins the M1 at Junction 23A. The church at Breedon-on-the-Hill is a prominent landmark.

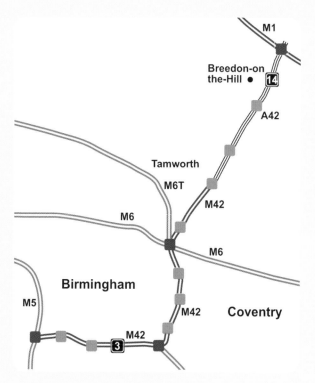

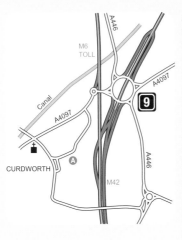

At the junction head for Curdworth. At the first roundabout go first left and after a few yards take a narrow road signed Furlong Lane to the left. Follow the lane through this picturesque village and go left at the bottom marked Beehive Lane. The pub is at the end on the left. Follow the signs to get back to the motorway.

Ⓐ The Beehive

Beehive Lane, Curdworth, West Midlands
01675 470 223

Satnav
B76 9HG

Orders for food: Mondays - Wednesdays: Noon to 9.30pm. Thursdays - Saturdays: Noon to 10.00pm. Sundays: Noon to 8.00pm.

££

A no frills locals' pub which has had a makeover since it appeared briefly in the 1st Edition. The service was cheerful and a strong coffee arrived within minutes of my arrival, having driven down from Northumberland in continuous rain. There is a beer garden behind where dogs are welcome. A surprisingly peaceful environment.

For those driving north, take the A453 towards Castle Donington. Turn left at the T junction and head to Breedon. To continue north you will have to use the

A453 to join the M1 at Junction 23a. The reverse will apply for those coming from the north.

Places of interest

The Saxon Church, Breedon on the Hill - 3miles
Calke Abbey(1701) NT - 5miles
Staunton Harold Church (!665) NT - 5 Miles

Ⓐ The Three Horseshoes Satnav DE73 8AN

Main Road, Breedon-on-the-Hill, Derbys.
01332 695 129
www.thehorseshoes.com

Orders for food: Mondays to Saturdays: 11.30am to 2.00pm and 6.00pm to 9.00pm. Sundays: Noon to 3.00pm.

 ££

It was used by a farrier but Jennie has made it into a comfortable cheerful place with open spaces and lofty ceilings. The service is friendly and
if need be fast. It also sells farm produce (and local ice-cream) over the counter as well as some useful presents.

M48

M5 TO CHEPSTOW

JUNCTIONS **1** & **2**

The present M48 was the M4 when the first Severn Bridge was built.

With the increase in traffic it became necessary to build another bridge further down stream which then was called the M4 and the older section was renamed the M48.

It can sometimes be quicker to take the old route rather than the denser stream of traffic on the new section.

Both bridges are apt to be closed whenever there is a strong wind blowing.

Junction 2 is where you can turn off to visit Chepstow which is a charming old riverside town with its massive castle which had been the centre of early Norman rule in Wales.

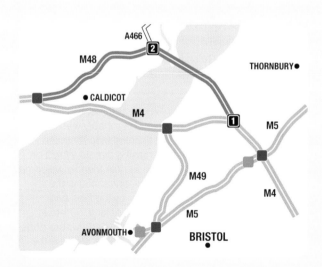

The Boars Head is just off the junction in the village of Aust. If you would like to stretch your legs you can go down to the river bank where the rotting piles of the old ferry crossing can still be seen.
For the White Hart take the B4461 towards Thornbury and then left in Elberton to Littleton.

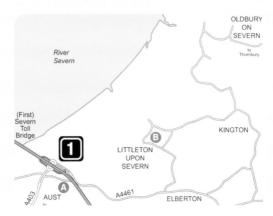

ⓐ Boar's Head

Main Road, Aust, S.Glos.
01454 632 278
www.marstonstaverns.co.uk
boarshead.aust@marstons.co.uk

Satnav
BS35 4AX

Orders for food: Daily: Noon to 3.00pm and 6.00pm to 9.00pm. Sundays: Noon to 4.00pm.

 £

A late 18th-century pub which probably was a coaching stop for those crossing over to Wales on the ferry. A friendly welcome to all, enhanced in the winter by log fires and home cooking. There is seating outside where dogs are welcome. Beware the beams.

B The White Hart

The Village, Littleton-upon-Severn, Glos.

Satnav
BS35 1NR

01454 412 275
www.whitehartbristol.com
whitehart@youngs.co.uk

Orders for food: Weekdays: Noon to 2.30pm and
6.00pm to 9.00pm. Saturdays: Noon to 2.30pm and
6.00pm to 9.00pm. Sundays: Noon to 8.00pm.

An old whitewashed pub on the outskirts of this small
village. Small rooms with a mix of old wooden furniture.
A restaurant, as well as bar meals being available.
Petanque in the garden for *les sportifs*. There is an
interesting scale-and-platt staircase dating from 1642.
A large orchard where customers can catch some
sunshine and fresh air.

M50

224   M5 to Ross-on-Wye

JUNCTIONS 1 TO 4

The M50 was one of the first motorways to be built and for some years remained in splendid isolation until joined to the M5. It was built to connect the Midlands with South Wales but only goes as far as Ross-on-Wye. It then continues as a dual-carriageway to Newport.

It is also a way of driving to Wales without paying the toll charges levied on the Severn Bridges!

There are plenty of places to see not too far from the motorway. Ross-on-Wye is a market town with interesting old buildings. Nearby is picturesque Symonds Yat where the river Wye winds through a gorge below the imposing ruins of Goodrich Castle.

To the south is the Forest of Dean, famous amongst other things for small family-owned coal mines which are still in private ownership.

To the west is the town of Monmouth with its medieval bridge and further on are the imposing ruins of Raglan Castle which was destroyed by Cromwell.

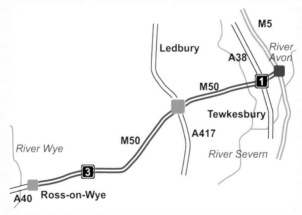

For the Fleet Inn and Village Inn in Twyning turn sharp left at the roundabout after you come off the motorway.

Ⓐ The Fleet Inn

Satnav
GL20 6FL

Fleet Lane, Twyning, Glos.
01684 274 020
www.thefleetattwyning.co.uk
enquiries@thefleetattwyning.co.uk

Orders for food: Monday to Friday: Noon to 9.30pm.
Saturdays & Sundays: Noon to 9.00pm

  ££

It has recently been substantially refurbished. Situated on the banks of the Avon you can watch the ducks swim (or walk). One of the girls can help you if you get stuck with the crossword..

ⓑ The Village Inn

Satnav
GL20 6DF

Twyning Green, Twyning, Glos.
01684 293 500
villageinn@fsmail.net

Orders for food: Monday to Saturday: Noon to 2.00pm
and 6.30pm to 9.00pm. Sundays: Noon to 4.00pm.

 ££

It was once a bakery, then a shop and Post Office, but is
now a pub in this picturesque village. There is a
secluded garden at the back or else you can sit outside
at the front watching the world go by. There is also a
Skittle Alley for rainy days but it has not seen action for
quite a long time. Plenty of atmosphere.

The Roadmaker is on the right on the Newent road, 300 yards from the junction. Continue on this road through Kilcot and the Kilcot Inn will be on the left. The Moody Cow is in Upton Bishop on the crossroads.

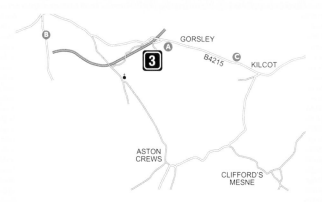

Ⓐ The Roadmaker Inn

Newent Road, Gorsley, Glos.

Satnav
HR9 7SW

01989 720 352
www.theroadmakerinn.co.uk
info@theroadmaker.co.uk

Orders for food: Monday to Saturday: 11.30am to 2.30pm and 6.00pm to 10.00pm. Sundays: 11.30am to 3.30pm and 6.00pm to 9.00pm.

££

It is owned by an ex-Ghurka and has been modernised. The service is discreet and friendly. The menu is half English at lunch and wholly Ghurkalese in the evening, which I thoroughly enjoyed.

Ⓑ Moody Cow

Satnav
HR9 7TT

Main Road, Upton Bishop, Herefordshire.
01989 780 470
www.moodycowpub.co.uk
dawn@moodycowpub.co.uk

Orders for food: Tuesday to Saturday: Noon to 2.30pm and 6.00pm to 9.00pm. Sundays: Noon to 3.00pm. No lunches on Mondays.

 £££

A Free House with individualistic décor. There is a fresco (as opposed to an alfresco) dining area near the bar and the main beamed dining room is in the converted barn. Outside a patio with tables and umbrellas. The food has a continental theme and is home cooked with fresh ingredients.

ⒸKilcot Inn

Satnav
GL18 1NA

Ross Road, Newent, Glos
01989 720 707
www.kilcotinn.com
info@kilcotinn.com

Orders for food: Daily: Breakfast: 9.00am to 11.30am. Lunch: Noon to 2.30pm. Dinner: 6.00pm to 9.30pm.

 £££

Substantially rebuilt and refurbished, it was opened in June 2011 and is owned by the family who produce Weston Cider. It has an imaginative menu supplemented by home grown vegetables. Sandwiches are however available. The four bedrooms above are new and comfortable. Outside there is seating and a rose garden. Pay heed to the notice "Duck yer Nut"

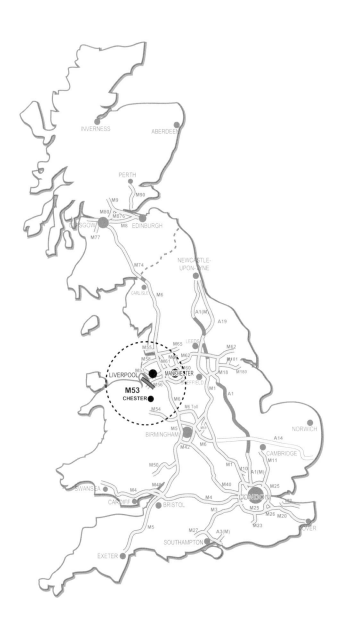

M53

BIRKENHEAD TO CHESTER M53

JUNCTIONS **1** TO **12**

This short 12-mile stretch of motorway passes through the densely industrialised area of Ellesmere Port as well as some pleasant wooded countryside. Port Sunlight is the home of soap and the Leverhulme house and art collection. There are apparently more millionaires in the Wirral than elsewhere in the UK excluding the London area.

At the other end of the motorway is Chester, still a walled city with medieval buildings and once the home base of the Roman XX (Victrix) Legion.

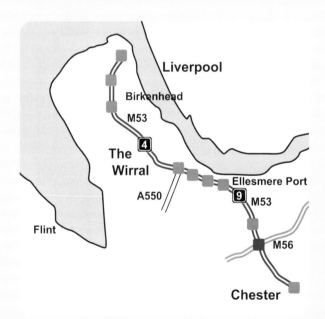

Take the B5137 from the junction towards Heswall. A mile after Brimstage bear to the right and after another mile turn right at the T-junction to Barnston. The Fox and Hounds does not do evening meals. The Ship, which is part of the same group, has 6 bedrooms and does breakfasts as well as evening meals.

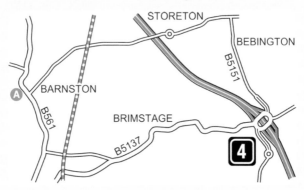

Ⓐ Fox and Hounds

Satnav
CH61 1BW

Barnston Road, Barnston, Wirral
0151 648 7685
www.the-fox-hounds.co.uk
info@the-fox-hounds.co.uk

Orders for food: Tuesdays-Fridays: Noon to 2.00pm and 5.00pm to 8.30pm. Sundays: Noon to 3.00pm. No evening meals on Sundays and Mondays.

£

Built in 1911 it is a well-ordered place with a dining area, a snug and a large bar area for bar meals. An eye-catching collection of 85 brass ashtrays, 115 horse brasses, police helmets and 30 flying ducks will keep you occupied or diverted whilst ordering.

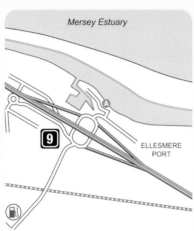

Just follow the signs to the Boat Museum, which is well worth a visit.

Places of interest
The Boat Museum

Ⓐ Jabula Restaurant

Satnav
CH65 4FW

South Pier Road, Ellesmere Port, S.Wirral
01513 551 163
www.jabularestaurant.co.uk
jabulainfo@btconnect.com
Orders for food: Daily: Noon to 2.30pm and 5.30pm to 9.00pm. Closed on Mondays.

£

A large airy eating area. It specialises in contemporary South African cooking such as springbok, ostrich or crocodile, served by friendly South African staff.

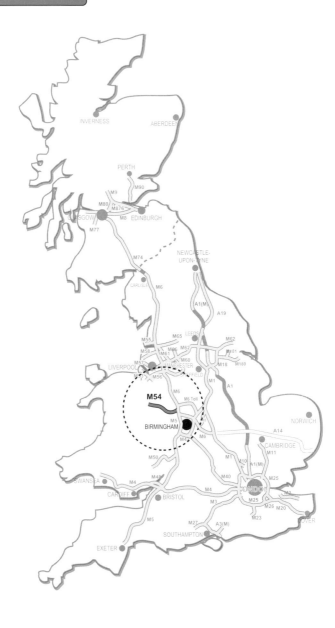

M54

BIRMINGHAM

JUNCTIONS 1 TO 7

This 23-mile stretch of motorway was opened in 1975 to link Birmingham to Shrewsbury and Wales.

After coming off the M6 it passes through pleasant farming countryside until the much vaunted Telford New Town, which is typical of 1960s planning – interminable tree-lined roads and roundabouts with sparse signing.

Beyond Telford it has been upgraded to dual carriageway to the other side of Shrewsbury.

The Ironbridge Gorge is the cradle of modern industry. Close by is medieval Much Wenlock with its Priory. To the west of Telford rises the Wrekin and beyond are the ruins of the Roman administrative town of Viroconium, now Wroxeter, with the remains of its massive public baths. Shrewsbury itself is one of the most attractive county towns in England with a wealth of old buildings.

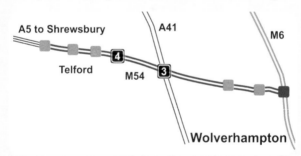

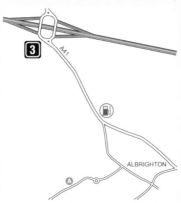

Take the A41 towards Wolverhampton. After 1.5 miles there is a road bearing right to Albrighton. Continue under a bridge and take the second right onto Bowling Green Laneand through a housing estate. Continue straight on at a roundabout down a lane. Take the first right and you will see the nursery ahead.

Places of interest

Weston Park (1671) HHA – 4 miles
Boscobel House (17thC) EH – 4 miles
Lilleshall Abbey EH – 11 miles
Air Museum, Shifnal – 1 mile

David Austin Roses

Satnav
WV7 3HB

Bowling Green Lane, Albrighton, Shrops.
01902 376 334
www.davidaustinroses.com
plantcentre@davidaustinroses.com

Orders for food: Daily: 9.30am to 4.30pm.

 ££

Many of you will have bought his world-famous roses but did you also know that you can have an excellent light lunch while pondering the future layout of your garden? Even I found myself selecting the odd rose shrub to buy.

Take the A442 towards Bridgnorth and Norton is about 8 miles to the south.

The Apley Farm Shop is more than 5 minutes but worth the extra time.

If you want a meal or a bed for the night the Hundred House Hotel is in the same village.

For those wanting a longer stay there are 3 holiday cottages on the banks of the Severn. Details from the Apley Farm Shop.

Places of interest

Ironbridge Gorge and museum – 5 miles

🅐 Apley Farm Shop

Satnav
TF11 9EF

Stockton Buildings, Norton, Shropshire
01952 730 345
www.apleyfarmshop.co.uk
enquiries@apleyfarmshop.com

Orders for food: Monday to Saturday: 9.30am to 5.00pm. Sundays: 10.00am to 3.00pm.

                    ££

A recently opened Farm Shop in a converted old dairy complex which is privately owned and sells its own produce. There is a separate café in the old cheese dairy which serves breakfasts and light lunches as well as teas. There is also a childrens' playbarn with suitable refreshments. A friendly welcome in a picturesque and genuinely rustic setting.

 **M54** **4** Telford East A464,
Kidderminster A442, Ironbridge

ⓑ Hundred House Hotel

Satnav
TF11 9EE

Bridgenorth Road, Norton, Shropshire.
01952 730 353
www.hundredhousehotel.co.uk
reservations@hundredhouse.co.uk

Orders for food: Daily: Noon to 2.30pm and 6.00pm
to 9.30pm. Breakfasts: Monday to Friday: 7.30am to
9.30am. Weekends: 8.00am to 10.00am.

      ££

Dating back to the 14th century, it was once a
courthouse and the stocks are still in place on the other
side of the road. It is now a friendly family hotel with
two dining areas and a bar. Good English, locally
sourced, food with a twist using their own home grown
herbs.

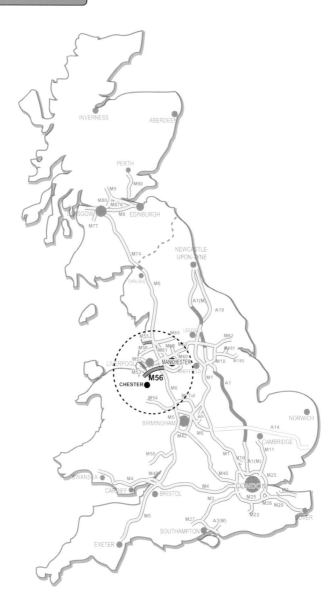

JUNCTIONS 1 TO 16

Some 37 miles long, it connects Manchester with the commuter areas of Cheshire as well as Chester and North Wales beyond.

It is not particularly attractive, but once over the intersection with the M6 (a complicated junction and badly signed) it gets better. At the end of the motorway it continues into Wales as a dual carriageway.

The historic city of Chester was once the base of the Roman XX (Victrix) Legion. It still has its medieval walls and was where the dramatist and architect Sir John Vanbrugh grew up.

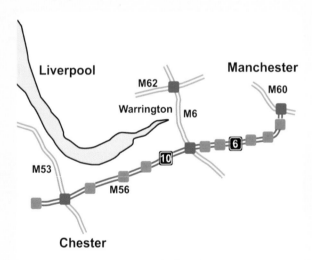

From the junction take the A538 towards Wilmslow. After going through the tunnel underneath the runway of Manchester Airport, the Honey Bee will be on your left.

The Honey Bee

Altrincham Road, Morley, Ches.
01625 526 511
www.vintageinn.co.uk/thehoneybeewilmslow

Satnav
SK9 4LT

Orders for food: Weekdays: Noon to 10.00pm.
Sundays: Noon to 9.30pm.

££

It started life privately as Oversley House until about 1950

when it became a residential home for the elderly. It must have been so comfortable that it was then converted into the Oversley House Hotel before assuming its present mantle as a comfortable inn.

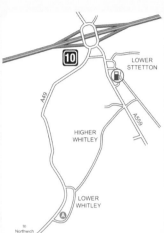

Take the A49 towards
Northwich. The
Chetwode Arms is three
miles south in Lower
Whitley and take a
sharp left beyond the
outskirts of the village

Places of interest
Arley Hall (19thC) HHA – 6 miles
Belmont Hall Pte - 6 miles

Chetwode Arms

Satnav
WA4 4EN

Street Lane, Lower Whitley, Ches.
01925 730 203
www.chetwodearms.org
info@chetwodearms.co.uk

Orders for food: Weekdays: 5.00pm to 9.00pm.
Saturdays: 3.30pm to 10.00pm. Sundays: 2.30pm to
5.30pm.

£££

A brick-built former coaching
inn, which now provides
individual service for the
discerning diner in three
former bar parlours with open
fires. The co-owner is
Austrian so from time to time
you may be lucky to have
Schnitzel. Otherwise you will
have to be more than content
with the high quality fare.

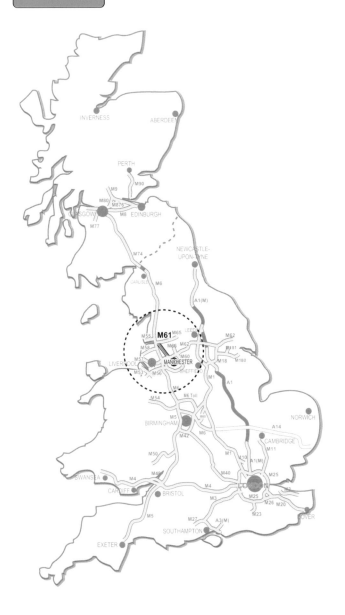

M61

JUNCTIONS **1** TO **9**

A useful motorway for those living around Manchester who are going to or coming from the Lake District or the north. It is also an alternative for motorists arriving over the Pennines on the M62 to connect with the M6 going north. Apart from that, there is little that can be said for it.

About the only redeeming feature is the sight of the Pennines to the east looming over the outer suburbs of Manchester and Bolton. The place names in the area, such as Whittle-le-Woods or Bottom o' the' Moor have a certain charm.

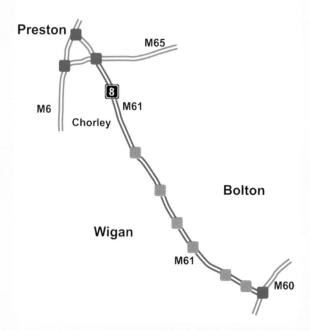

The Red Cat requires concentration as you have to
drive past it and then come round behind it. The
Dressers Arms is in Whelton and is easy to see.

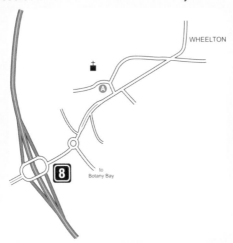

Ⓐ **Red Cat**

Satnav
PR6 8LL

Blackburn Road, Whittle-le-Woods, Lancs.
01257 263 966
www.theredcat.co.uk
enquiries@theredcat.co.uk

Orders for food: Wednesday to Saturday: Noon to
2.00pm and 6.00pm to 9.30pm. Sundays: Noon to
8.00pm. Closed Mondays and Tuesdays.

££

There has been an inn
here since 1805. It is
a cheerful place,
specialising in modern
British food served in the
flagstoned eating areas
and outside.

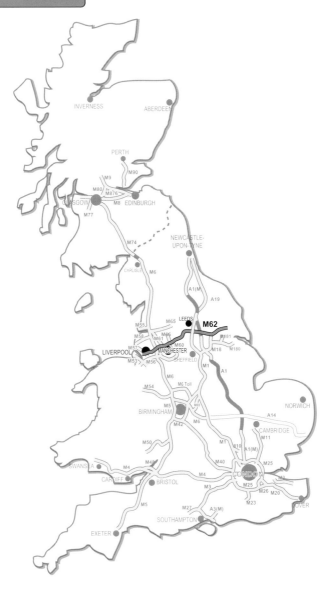

LIVERPOOL TO HULL

JUNCTIONS 1 TO 38

One of the few motorways which run laterally across the country. It is 108 miles long and was completed in 1976 to link the ports of Liverpool and Hull. It does not lend itself to gastronomic feasts.

It is divided into two sections.

LIVERPOOL TO HUDDERSFIELD

JUNCTIONS 6 TO 24

This part, from Liverpool to beyond Manchester, is not pretty. However once past Junction 21 it rises up into the Pennines. Junction 22, which at 1221 ft (372m), is the highest point of any motorway in the UK. It could also be a remote spot for picnics near the top. The motorway then descends into the industrial areas of Huddersfield and Bradford.

Junction 22 is the highest junction in the country and is 1221 feet or 372 metres above sea level. Take the A672 towards Ripponden. The Turnpike is about three miles on the left of the road. The views are stunning, marred only by the street lights along the motorway.

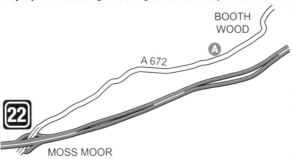

BOOTH WOOD

A 672

Ⓐ

22

MOSS MOOR

Ⓐ The Turnpike

Satnav
HX6 4QT

Oldham Road, Rishworth, W.Yorks.
01422 822 789
www.turnpikeinn.com
bookit@turnpikeinn.com

Orders for food: Monday to Saturday: Noon to 9.00pm.
Sundays: Noon to 8.00pm. Breakfast: 9.00am to 11am.

   £

A simple wayside pub, which may have been the toll for the turnpike road. Apart from bar meals,

breakfast can be had from 9.00am onwards. There is a good view over the reservoir to the Pennines and the isolated farmhouse between the two carriageways of the M62.

LEEDS TO HULL

JUNCTIONS 25 TO 38

Not the most attractive part of England as it passes through the industrial areas south of Leeds.

Once past the intersection with the A1(M) and the famous Ferrybridge Power Station, the countryside becomes flat and level intersected by drainage ditches and fens excepting the odd slag heap or power station.

The high bridge over the River Ouse gives views of the tower of the Minster at Howden which is impressive and the inland port of Goole, made visible by the cranes.

The motorway ceases just short of Brough, an old Roman town which was the ferry point for those crossing over the Humber in those days. It continues as a dual carriageway to Hull and the ferry terminals for Rotterdam and Zeebrugge.

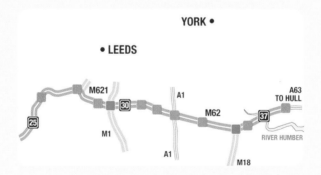

Take the road to Brighouse. After less than half a mile there is a road to the right. Up the hill and bear to the left. The Black Horse is on the left.

 **The Black Horse Inn**

Satnav
HD6 4HJ

Towgate, Clifton, W.Yorks.
01484 713 862
www.blackhorseclifton.co.uk
mail@blackhorseclifton.co.uk

Orders for food: Weekdays: Noon to 2.30pm and 5.30pm to 9.30pm. Sundays: Noon to 8.00pm.
Breakfasts: Weekdays: 7.00am to 10.00am.
Weekends: 8.00am to 10.00am but book in before.

£££

Once a 17th-century inn it is now a well-furnished, friendly family-run hostelry. There are two dining rooms and plenty of space with an efficient bar. A well-deserved reputation for comfort and ease in this part of the world.

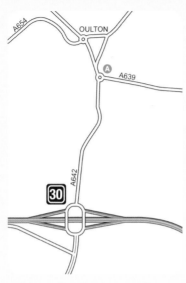

The Three Horse Shoes is on the right just beyond the first roundabout on the A642 to Leeds.
It is conspicuous by the colourful hanging baskets.

Three Horse Shoes

Satnav
LS26 8JU

16 Leeds Road, Oulton, W.Yorks
0113 282 2370
www.threehorseshoesoulton.co.uk
info@threehorseshoesoulton.co.uk

Orders for food: Daily: 11.30am to 9.00pm.
Sundays: Noon to 8.00pm.

££

A popular place, especially for those living nearby. It has won Best Pub for Flowers in Yorkshire for the past three years and the hanging baskets are a wonder to behold. Friendly and quick service even though the place may be full of folk.

M62 | **37** Howden A64 Selby York A63 Bridlington

NORTH HOWDEN

B1228

A

HOWDEN

A614

37

Howden was once famous for being one of Europe's largest horse fairs and where the Bishop of Durham's Summer Palace was situated. With the Dissolution of the Monasteries Howden declined and until some thirty years ago it had become a one horse town. Thanks to the generosity of the Monument Trust the Great Hall of the Palace was rescued and restored and since then the town has become a picturesque market town again dominated by the Minster.

 Bowmans Hotel

Bridgegate, Howden, Yorks
01430 430 805
clemndunn@aol.com

Satnav
DN14 7AE

Orders for food: Weekdays: 5.00pm to 9.00pm.
Saturdays: Noon to 7.00pm. Sundays: Noon to 3.00pm.
Breakfasts: 7.00am to 9.00am.

££

An ex-coaching house called the Nags Head until 1834. It was extended in 1864 when Howden hosted the Yorkshire Show. Large open plan bar with three dining areas. A friendly Yorkshire welcome.

254   M62 Liverpool to Hull

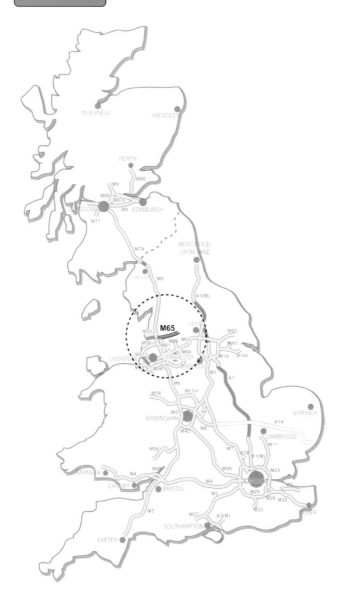

PRESTON TO COLNE

 **M65**

JUNCTIONS 1 TO 27

For many years the M65 was a short isolated stretch from Blackburn to Colne. It has now been completed to link up with the M6 at Preston and end at Junction 13 at Nelson.
From there you will have to find your way to Skipton and on to Harogate or Keighley and Bradford.

There is not much to say about it except that you are driving through the last remaining vestiges of the Lancashire cotton industry with huge palatial factories of Italianate architecture.

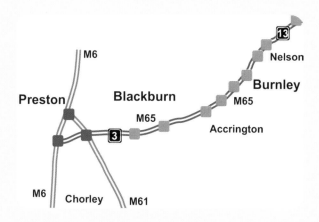

The roundabout at the end of the slip-road could be confusing.

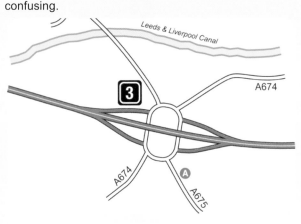

Places of interest
Hoghton Tower (1100-1565) HHA – 3 miles

 Ristorante Alghero

Bolton Road, Withnell, Lancs.
01254 202 222
www.algheros.co.uk
info@algheros.co.uk

Satnav
PR6 8BP

Orders for food: Daily: 5.00pm to 10.00pm.
Sundays: Noon to 9.30pm.

£££

As the name implies, this is a Sardinian restaurant which has a good local reputation and a friendly atmosphere.

As you come off the motorway to Barrowford the Thatch and Thistle is on your left.

Thatch and Thistle

Satnav
BB9 7TZ

Surrey Road, Nelson, Lancs.
01282 615 215
4890@greeneking.co.uk

Orders for food: Daily: 11.00am to 9.00pm.

££

A modern thatched roadhouse which has an American flavour. Large open areas for eating, a pool table for amusement and open (gas) fires for warmth. The welcome is friendly and the staff were very helpful to me.

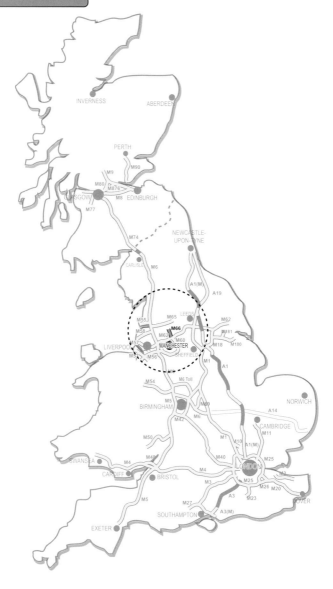

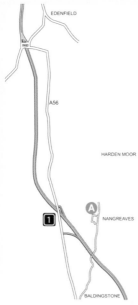

Going North come off at the Junction and left on the A56 to Bury. After 1½ miles turn left at the traffic lights and take the Old Road up the hill to Nangreaves which is a cobbled road throughout. The Lord Raglan is to the left as you get to the top of the hill, which is a dead end.

To continue north return to the traffic lights and drive up the A56 to Edenfield. Driving south, you will have to get off at Edenfield but you can rejoin the M66 at Junction 1.

Ⓐ The Lord Raglan

Mount Pleasant, Nr Bury, Lancs.
0161 764 6680
www.lordraglannangreaves.co.uk

Satnav **BL9 6SP**

Orders for food: Monday to Thursday: Noon to 2.00pm and 6.00pm to 9.00pm. Fridays: Noon to 2.00pm and 5.00pm to 9.00pm. Saturdays: Noon to 9.00pm. Sundays: Noon to 8.00pm.

   £

It is aptly named Mount Pleasant as you will find yourself on top of the hills in rural Lancashire with a view of moorland and the Pennines. It has been in the same family for three generations so it has a cheerful atmosphere with a friendly staff. The menu and the moorland air make for a pleasant stopover.

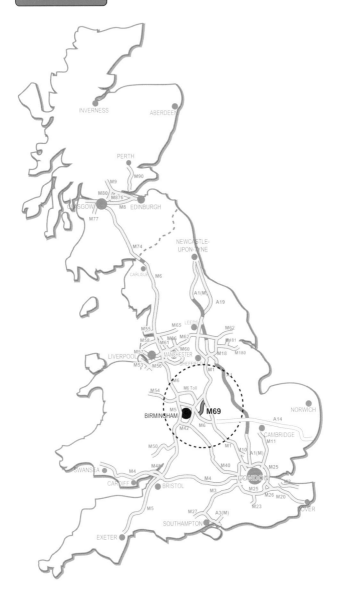

🛣 M69

JUNCTIONS **1** TO M1

The motorway was built in the mid 1970s to give direct access between Coventry and Leicester. It is comparatively little used so is useful to those who use the M1 or M40 as a means of driving north or south.

The junction with the M1 is rather abrupt as a result of a decision at the time not to make it into a proper clover-leaf exit as the volume of traffic would not warrant the expense. It will now be very expensive to reverse the decision.

The building of the motorways has had the curious effect of isolating corners of the countryside to create rural areas of calm, such as the part around Bosworth Field ("…my kingdom for a horse"), which has now been proved to be in the wrong place!

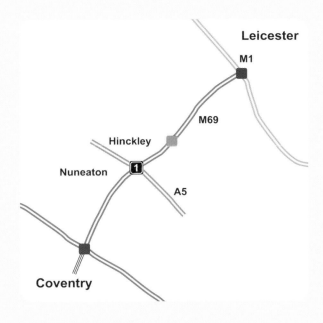

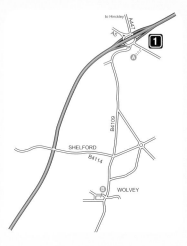

Barnacles Restaurant is easily found off the A5, the old Roman Watling Street.
For the Blue Pig take the Wolvey Road. In the village there is a modern pub and a post office on the right and a sharp turning just beyond it. Turn right and the Blue Pig is down the road on the left.

Places of interest
Bosworth Battlefield (1485) – 8 miles

 # Barnacles Restaurant

Satnav
LE10 3JA

Watling Street, Hinckley, Warks.
01455 633 220
www.barnaclesrestaurant.co.uk
enq@barnaclesrestaurant.co.uk

Orders for food: Weekdays: Noon to 2.00pm and 6.00pm to 9.00pm. Saturdays: 6.00pm to 9.30pm. Sundays: Closed.

£££

A privately owned restaurant in pleasant grounds with a lake. It specialises in fish and there is a separately owned fish shop next to the restaurant. Dogs are not welcomed and there are no special facilities for children.

B The Blue Pig

Hall Road, Wolvey, Leics.
01455 220 256
www.thebluepigpub.co.uk
enquiries@thebluepig.co.uk

Satnav
LE10 3LG

Orders for food: Mondays to Fridays: Noon to 3.00pm
and 5.00pm to 9.00pm. Saturdays: Noon to 9.00pm.
Sundays: Noon to 5.00pm.

                                    ££

An old coaching inn dating from the 15th century with
exposed masonry walls and low beams with quips such
as "Now Good Digestion wait on Appetite & Health on
Both". There is a restaurant and a bar serving real ales.
Home cooked specials prepared by Fran who comes
from Airdrie. Dog biscuits are free for well behaved dogs.

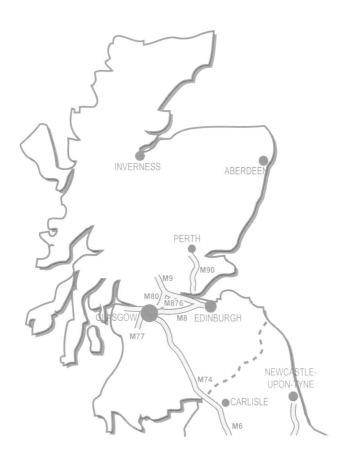

INVERNESS

ABERDEEN

PERTH

M9

M90

M80

M876

M8 EDINBURGH

GLASGOW

M77

M74

NEWCASTLE-
UPON-TYNE

CARLISLE

M6

SCOTLAND

Scotland does extend a warm welcome to visitors and even Sassenachs, but the motorway user gets the impression that the Scots have forgotten the art of hospitality to the passing traveller.

This could be due to the fact that the new motorways, except for the M74, do not follow the old coaching routes which is equally true in England.

There are some excellent exceptions to the rule, but there were a lot of places which could not be included. On the M8 for example, from Edinburgh to Glasgow there is only one place worthy of being mentioned, but that is too difficult to find.

The most tedious aspect of the Scottish motorways is the system of linked junctions. It might save money, but it generates unnecessary driving on minor roads. This might improve if Scotland decides to go it alone.

M9

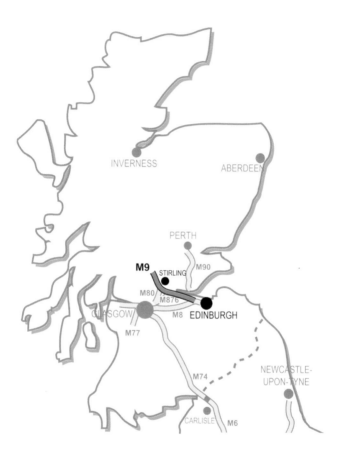

EDINBURGH TO STIRLING

JUNCTIONS TO

This links Edinburgh with Stirling and beyond. It is also useful if the Forth Road Bridge is closed because of high winds.

Beware of the the linked junctions as once off the motorway it will take time to regain it.

It passes through agricultural country, and old shale heaps. There are some fine examples of Renaissance architecture such as Linlithgow Palace and Stirling Castle.

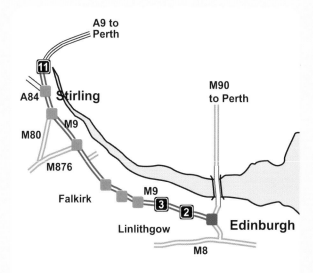

M9 | **2/3** | Forth Road Bridge (A4904)
Linlithgow A803, Bo'ness A904

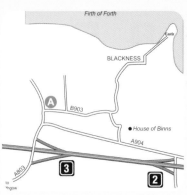

Like most of the junctions these are linked together, depending upon the direction of travel. There are alternative places in Linlithgow to suit most requirements.

Places of interest
Hopetoun House (1699 & 1721) HHA – 4 miles
The House of the Binns (17thC) NTS – 1 miles
Blackness Castle (14th & 16thC) HS – 3 miles
Linlithgow Palace (Burnt 1746) HS – 2 miles

Ⓐ Champany Inn

Satnav
EH49 7LU

Champany, W. Lothian
01506 834 532
www.champany.com
reception@champany.com

Orders for food: Daily: Noon to 2.00pm and 6.30pm to 10.00pm. Saturday: Noon to 10.00pm. Sunday: 12.30am to 10.00pm.

£££

It was once a farmhouse where Mary Queen of Scots used to come over from Linlithgow to have picnics in the country, hence the name. Outside seating for hot days and a bistro to suit the more hurried motorist. It is noted for Aberdeen Angus beef.

After coming off the roundabout, drive towards the outskirts of the Bridge of Allan. Turn right just before the bridge with a high wooded bluff on the other side of the river. The Inn is to the right.

Places of interest

Doune Castle (14thC) HS – 3 miles
Stirling Castle (13thC & Renaissance) HS – 5 miles
Argyll's Lodging (17thC) HS – 5 miles
The Wallace Monument – 2 miles

A The Old Bridge Inn

Inverallen Road, Bridge of Allen, Stirlings.
01786 833 335
www.oldbridgeinn.co.uk
Orders for food: Daily: Noon to 10.00pm

Satnav
FK9 4JA

££

The Inn was originally surrounded by mills and by Willie's brewery. The interior has been stripped out to make a larger area with rough stone walls and timber panelling to form a comfortable restaurant/bar, where local fish and salmon from the Tay is also served. A bell from a Glasgow church is used to signal last orders.

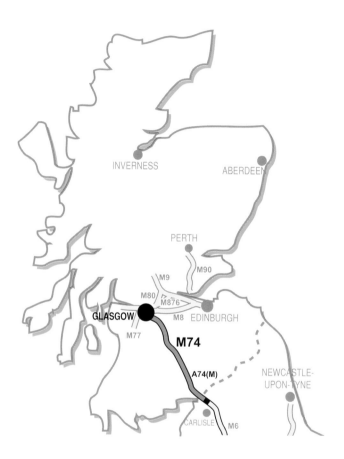

INVERNESS

ABERDEEN

PERTH

M90

M9

M80

M876

GLASGOW

M8 EDINBURGH

M77

M74

A74(M)

NEWCASTLE-
UPON-TYNE

CARLISLE M6

GLASGOW TO CARLISLE M74

JUNCTIONS 4 TO 22

The A74 has now been rebuilt to motorway standard throughout.

North of Junction 13 it is the M74, but south to the Border it is still the A74(M).

The section of dual carriageway between Scotland and England has now been upgraded to motorway standard.

There is almost nowhere south of Glasgow where you can stop to find a decent meal. However, there are some impressive buildings to see such as Bothwell Castle, Chatelherault, Cadzow Castle and Craigneathen.

The town of Moffat off Junction 15 is interesting and has a variety of places to eat and sleep.

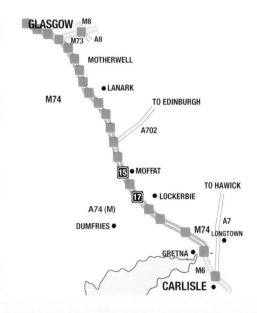

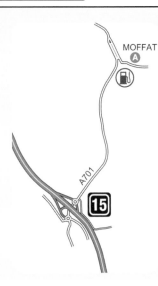

Moffat is an historic market town and on one of the many roads to Edinburgh. It has some fine buildings and hostelries so worth the short detour to see it. From the junction take the A701 to Selkirk and in the town right again on the A708 to Galashiels. Brodies is 100 yards ahead of you.

 Brodies

Satnav
DG10 9EB

Altrive Place, Holm Street, Moffat, Dumfriesshire.
01683 222 870
www.brodiesofmoffat.co.uk
whatscooking@brodiesofmoffat.co.uk

Orders for food: Daily: 10.00am to 10.00pm.
Check the website for times in winter.

££

A bright, clean and bustling restaurant and wine bar. A good lunch menu with fresh home cooked food at a reasonable price and you can also have a late breakfast. As we left several families were tucking into delicious looking afternoon teas.

An easy junction, you can see the hotel from the motorway.

Places of interest
Lochmaben Castle (15thC) HS – 4 miles

 Dryfesdale Hotel

Satnav
DG11 2SF

Nr. Lockerbie, Dumfriesshire
01576 202 427
www.dryfesdalehotel.co.uk
reception@dryfesdalehotel.co.uk

Orders for food: Daily: Noon to 2.00pm and 6.00pm to 9.00pm. Sundays: Noon to 2.00pm and 6.00pm to 8.00pm.

£££

The house was built in the late 17th century as the Manse and was converted into a hotel in the early 1900s. It has a restaurant and a bar catering for lunches and dinners, and bar meals are available for those in a hurry. Telephone beforehand.

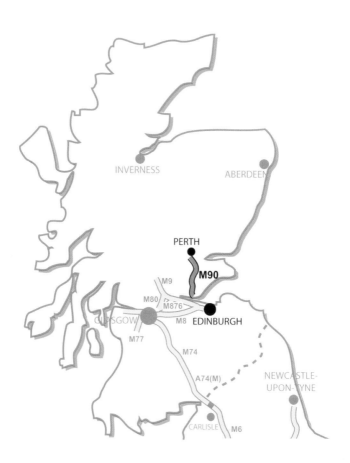

JUNCTIONS 1 TO 11

An interesting motorway which starts at the Forth Road Bridge and ends in Perth.

Loch Leven was where Mary Queen of Scots was imprisoned. Beyond Glenfarg the motorway descends to the Bridge of Earn. Behind Moncrieffe Hill are the outskirts of Perth and beyond to the north can be seen the distant outline of the Highlands.

On the way, there are castles such as Elcho to be seen and to the east is Abernethy where William the Conqueror took the personal submission of King Malcolm Canmore in 1072.

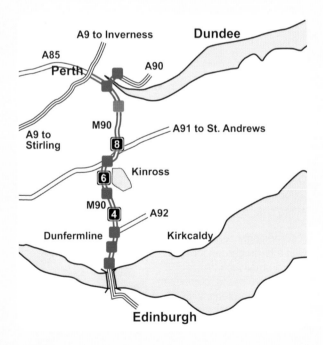

The private road to The Grouse and Claret is opposite the Esso Filling Station. If it is full, there are at least four hotels in Kinross.

Places of interest
Loch Leven Castle (14thC) HS – 2 miles
Kinross House Garden (17thC) HHA – 1 mile

 **Grouse and Claret**

Heatheryford, Kinross
01577 864 212
www.grouseandclaret.com
grouseandclaret@lineone.net

Satnav
KY13 0NQ

Orders for food: Daily: Noon to 2.00pm and 6.30pm to 9.00pm. Sundays: No evening meals. Mondays: Closed.

££

A surprisingly peaceful spot, with a large garden looking onto a small loch. An imaginative menu, combining Scottish ingredients with an Eastern twist, in a comfortable restaurant with a bar.

Those of us who had to endure the steep twisting road before the advent of the motorway will remember the Bein Inn. The old B996 is still there but access is from Junction 8 or else at the bottom at Junction 9.

 The Bein Inn

Main Road, Glenfarg, Perthshire
01577 830 216
www.beininn.com
enquiries@beininn.com

Satnav
PH2 9PY

Orders for food: Daily: Noon to 9.00pm in summer. In winter: Noon to 2.00pm and 5.00pm to 9.00pm. Breakfasts: From 8.00am

££

Set in a tree-covered dip by the old road it was well known to those travelling north or south. It is now family-owned and is an efficient, well-run hotel with a good reputation for food. A cheerful atmosphere.

This is not a comprehensive list and is based on the information given. However the times vary from place to place and it is advisable when planning your route to check beforehand.

A1	-	Elton	Loch Fyne Restaurant	01832 280298
	-	Caunton	Caunton Beck	01636 636793
	50	Pickhill	Nag's Head	01845 567391
A14	47	Norton	Norton Dog	01359 230440
M1	14	Mulsoe	Carrington Arms	01908 318050
	16	Flore	Bliss Tearoom	01327 342283
	19	Catthorpe	Manor Farm Shop	01788 869002
M4	17	St Quintin	Stanton Manor Hotel	01666 837552
	18	Dyrham	Tollgate Teashop	01225 891585
M5	7	Whittington	The Swan	01905 351361
	27	Uffculme	The Old Well	01884 840873
	30	Topsham	Darts Farm	01392 878200
M6	19	Tabley	The Windmill	01565 625885
	27	Wrightington	White Lion	01257 425977
	36	Sizergh	Sizergh Barn	01539 560426
	38	Orton	Kennedys	01539 624781
M20	7	Detling	Black Horse	01622 737185
M25	6	Godstone	Green Rooms	01883 740407
M27	1	Brook	Bell Hotel	02380 812214
M40	6	Tetsworth	The Swan	01844 281182
M50	3	Kilcot	Kilcot Inn	01989 720707
M54	3	Albrighton	David Austin Roses	01902 376334
	4	Norton	Hundred House Hotel	01952 580240
M62	22	Rishworth	Turnpike	01422 822789

England and Wales

England and Wales

England and Wales

A1

16	Peterborough Cathedral - 4m	
17	Elton Hall & Gdns HHA - 3m	01832 280468
45	Bramham Park HHA - 2m	01937 846000
48	Isurium Roman Town - 2m	
48	Newby Hall HHA - 8m	01423 322583

A3(M)

2	Stansted Park HHA - 1m	02392 413432

A14

2	Lamport Hall HHA - 4m	01604 686272
2	Kelmarsh Hall HHA - 4m	01604 686543
2	Cottesbrooke Hall & Gdns HHA - 8m	01604 505808
12	Lyveden New Bield NT - 7m	01832 205358
42	Ickworth House NT - 3m	01284 735720

M1

14	Bletchley Park Pte - 6m	01908 640404
19	Stanford Hall HHA - 2m	01788 861540
29	Hardwick Hall EH - 2m	01246 850430
29	Bolsover Castle EH - 1m	01246 822844
29	Sutton Scarsdale Hall EH - 1m	01246 822400
29	Chatsworth HHA - 15m	01246 582204
29	Haddon Hall HHA - 17m	01629 812855
37	Cannon Hall, Barnsley MBC - 2m	01226 790427

M3

4A	Napoleon III's Mausoleum, Farnborough Pte - 3m	
4A	Airborne Forces Museum - 4m	
5	Old Basing House, Hants C.C. - 5m	01256 467294
7	The Grange EH - 8m	01424 775705

M4

11	Stratfield Saye HHA - 5m	01256882694
11	Silchester (site of Calleva Atrebartum) - 7m	
12	Engelfield House Garden HHA - 3m	0118 9302504
12	Basildon Park NT - 7m	0118 9843040
13	Highclere Castle HHR - 6m	01635 253210
14	Ashdown House NT - 9m	01793 762209
17	Bowood House HHA - 6m	01249 812102
17	Lacock Abbey NT - 7m	01249 730459
17	Corsham Court HHA - 9m	01249 701610
18	Dyrham Park NT - 2m	01179 372501
18	Horton Court NT - 5m	01179 372501

M5

5	Hanbury Hall NT - 4m	01527 821214
9	Tewkesbury Abbey - 1m	
13	Wildfowl Ctre (Slimbridge) - 5m	01453 891900
23	Glastonbury Abbey - 13m	
24	Maunsel House HHA - 7m	01278 661076
25	Hestercombe Gdns HHA - 4m	01823 413923
26	Cothay Manor & Gdns HHA - 4m	01823 672283
27	Knightshayes Court NT - 6m	01884 257381

M6

17	Little Moreton Hall NT - 6m	01260 272018
18	Capesthorne Hall HHA - 11m	01625 861221
19	Arley Hall & Gdns HHA - 5m	01565 777353
19	Tatton Park NT - 3m	01625 374400
19	Tabley House - Univ. of M'chstr - 2m	01565 750151
36	Levens Hall & Gdns HHA - 4m	01539 560321
36	Sizergh Castle NT - 5m	01539 560951
38	Roman Fort, Low Borrowbridge - 3m	
39	Shap Abbey EH - 3m	

M40

12	Compton Verney CVH Trust - 4m	01926 645500
12	Heritage Motor Museum - 1m	01926 641188
12	Upton House NT - 9m	01295 670266
12	Edgehill Battlefield - 4m	
15	Charlecote Park NT - 7m	01789 470277

M42

14	The Saxon Church, Breedon-on-the-Hill - 3m	
14	Calke Abbey NT - 5m	01332 863822
14	Staunton Harold Church NT - 5m	01332 863822

M50

1	Tewkesbury Abbey - 3m	01684 850959
2	Eastnor Castle HHA - 5m	01531 633160

M54

3	Weston Park HHA - 4M	01952 852100
3	Boscobel House EH - 4m	01902 850244
3	Air Museum, Shifnal	01902 376200
3	Lilleshall Abbey EH - 11m	01216 256820
4	Ironbridge Gorge - 5m	01952 435900

M56

10	Arley Hall HHA - 6m	01565 777353
10	Belmont Hall Pte - 6m	01606 891235

M65

3	Hoghton Tower HHA - 3m	01254 852986

M69

1	Bosworth Battle Field - 8m	

Scotland

M9

2/3	Hopetoun House HHA - 4m	0131 3312451
2/3	The House of Binns NTS - 1m	01506 834255
2/3	Blackness Castle HS - 3m	01506 834807
2/3	Linlithgow Palace HS - 2m	01506 842896
11	Doune Castle HS - 3m	01786 841742
11	Stirling Castle HS - 5m	01786 450000

M74

17   Lochmaben Castle HS - 4m

M90

6   Loch Leven Castle HS - 2m (by water)   01577 862670

Reader's Suggestions

If you know of a place which should be included or if there has been a change of ownership which needs an amendment or deletion, then please let us know.

If your suggestion is included in the next edition we will send you a complimentary copy.

Your name and address...
....
....
Telephone..

I would suggest that the following entry be included/ amended/deleted.
Name...
Motorway..........Junction.....Village...
..................Details...
....
....
....
....
....
....

By e-mail to **info@cheviotbooks.co.uk** or by post to

Cheviot Books
High Street
Fifield
Oxon
OX7 6HD

Reader's Suggestions

If you know of a place which should be included or if there has been a change of ownership which needs an amendment or deletion, then please let us know.

If your suggestion is included in the next edition we will send you a complimentary copy.

Your name and address...

....

....

Telephone..

I would suggest that the following entry be included/ amended/deleted.

Name...

Motorway..........Junction.....Village.......................................

..................Details...

....

....

....

....

....

....

By e-mail to **info@cheviotbooks.co.uk** or by post to

Cheviot Books
High Street
Fifield
Oxon
OX7 6HD

Reader's Suggestions

If you know of a place which should be included or if there has been a change of ownership which needs an amendment or deletion, then please let us know.

If your suggestion is included in the next edition we will send you a complimentary copy.

Your name and address...
....
....
Telephone...

I would suggest that the following entry be included/ amended/deleted.

Name...
Motorway..........Junction.....Village.......................................
..................Details...
....
....
....
....
....
....
....

By e-mail to **info@cheviotbooks.co.uk** or by post to

Cheviot Books
High Street
Fifield
Oxon
OX7 6HD

Reader's Suggestions

If you know of a place which should be included or if there
has been a change of ownership which needs an
amendment or deletion, then please let us know.

If your suggestion is included in the next edition we will
send you a complimentary copy.

Your name and address...
....
....
Telephone...

I would suggest that the following entry be included/
amended/deleted.
Name...
Motorway..........Junction.....Village.......................................
.................Details...
....
....
....
....
....
....

By e-mail to **info@cheviotbooks.co.uk** or by post to

Cheviot Books
High Street
Fifield
Oxon
OX7 6HD